THE PEBBLE ROUTE

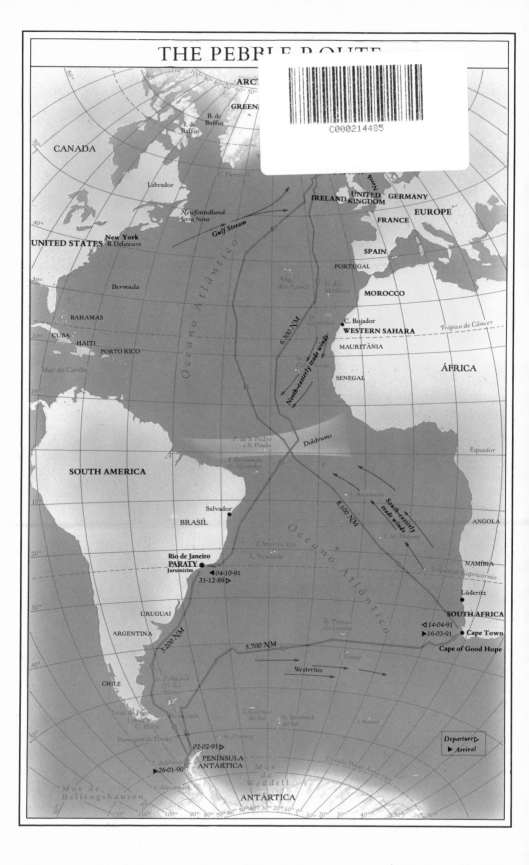

66

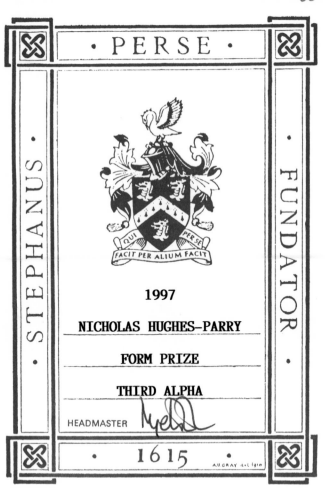

BETWEEN TWO POLES

Amyr Klink

Translated by Lucia Villares

BLOOMSBURY

First published in Brazil as *Paratti: Entre Dois Pólos* in 1992
This edition published 1995
Copyright © by Amyr Klink
Translation copyright 1995 by Lucia Villares
The moral right of the author and translator have been asserted

Bloomsbury Publishing Plc, 2 Soho Square, London W1V 6HB

A CIP catalogue record for this book is available from the British Library
ISBN 0 7475 1972 2

10   9   8   7   6   5   4   3   2   1

Typeset by Hewer Text Composition Services, Edinburgh
Printed in Great Britain by Clays Ltd, St Ives plc

Photographs by Amyr Klink, Ashraf Klink, Fausto Chermont and Audichromo
Editora

Maps by Sírio B. Cançado

Then fancies flee away
I'll care not what men say
I'll labour night and day
To be a pilgrim.

John Bunyan

CONTENTS

Introduction   ix

1   The Blue Schooner   1
2   Boats with No Sea   11
3   Happy Ships   19
4   Departure   37
5   In the Land of the Albatross   47
6   Red Ice   57
7   Square-eyed   67
8   Time Travellers   83
9   On the Far Side of the Ice   101
10 The Fragmented Bay   117
11 See You Later, *Rapa Nui*!   133
12 The Green Flash   151
13 Uncrossable Capes   163
14 Gathering the Pebbles   177
    Acknowledgments   199
    Bibliography   201
    A Note on the Author   203

INTRODUCTION

Henry the Navigator has much to answer for. The achievements of the fifteenth-century Portuguese prince who sent his sailors forth to carve sea-paths through the unknown world have left an unsatisfied hunger in the Portuguese-speaking soul. Take this ancient, mystic impulse of Portuguese navigators to seek out their *ne plus ultra*, and mix it with a truly modern passion for logistics, the art of conquering every foreseeable challenge of the elements through intelligence and foresight rather than with bravery, luck or brute force. Then you will begin to glimpse the motivations behind the voyages of Amyr Klink.

Born in Brazil but of mixed Lebanese and Swedish ancestry, Amyr blends the technological, environmental concerns of our times with a more ancient *wanderlust*. These two elements are so entwined it is difficult to know how much of his spirit belongs to the past, and how much to the future. One thing is certain: flowing waters and not dry land are his realm. Even his chosen home, the colonial-era port town of Paraty on the coast near Rio de Janeiro, is a little Venice, where high tides flood the cobbled streets, creating the illusion that its baroque churches are afloat. As a very small boy Amyr would be sent by canoe through these flooded streets to fetch bread from the baker, a prelude to progressively more demanding expeditions that have taken him ever further from Paraty, the home to which he always returns. At the age of twelve he rowed his small canoe for two hours to seek help for his brother and a friend who were stranded on a small island offshore. The canoe was repeatedly swamped by waves. Using tricks learned from local fishermen, he kept on paddling to arrive at the quayside in Paraty, soaked to the skin and teeth chattering, but possessed of a sense of achievement he will never forget. From then on, long journeys were to be a constant obsession for this young man, with a growing library of nautical adventurers and growing confidence in his own abilities: he sailed 1,000 miles in a small, open catamaran, and then another 1,200 miles down tributaries of the Amazon.

In September 1984, Amyr completed an extraordinary solo voyage across the Atlantic, rowing from Namibia to Bahia in northern Brazil in a tiny cockleshell of a boat. This feat was made all the more extraordinary by the fact that one of his wrists had been seriously damaged in an accident. Overcoming indifference and active discouragement on both sides of the Atlantic, he proved that by using the discoveries of the earliest navigators he could make nature work for, rather than against him. By carefully planning a route that took full advantage of the Benguela and South Equatorial currents to sweep him along for 4,000 miles, Amyr was sufficiently in control of his destiny during that three-month voyage across the Atlantic to savour the true purpose of travel: to observe, to wonder, to philosophise and to enjoy. Visited by seals, sharks, whales and gulls, Amyr organised a daily routine of meals, work, sleep and rest that allowed him to come to terms with the most dangerous aspect of his chosen path: solitude.

During this journey, which is described in *One Hundred Days Between the Sea and Sky*, Klink discovered his growing personal obsession with Antarctica through his admiration for Sir Ernest Shackleton, a master of logistics who never achieved the recognition of his rival Captain Scott – yet whose planning and leadership were of a far higher order. Amyr departed from Brazil for his Antarctic sojourn at the start of 1990. Like Shackleton's ship *Endurance*, his own *Paratii* was to be held fast in the ice. And like his predecessor, Amyr was not seeking 'death or glory' heroics, but simply the satisfaction of realising his own private dream and doing this with the minimum of fuss, though not without self-deprecating humour or comfort: the ice that held him fast also served to chill his birthday champagne.

Before he departed many warned him that he would be unable to cope with the danger and solitude of the long dark winter. Yet nothing would stop him. Having achieved his initial objective in the far south fourteen months later, Amyr then went on to show that he had departed from Brazil so well prepared that he could change his mind and simply keep on going due north, extending his voyage by over eight months to sail almost non-stop from one pole to the other. Between these two poles and between the lines of this intriguing travel book lies the answer to the question that draws readers to every tale of adventure: 'Why did he do it?'

In a world already so well travelled, Amyr's newest journey of discovery is to open up other minds. Just like the school of navigation established by Prince Henry at Sagres at the southernmost tip of Europe, the Brazilian has established his own school of navigation on an offshore island close to Paraty, aimed at restoring to his countrymen their forgotten seafaring heritage.

Lucia Villares, with assistance from Richard House

1

THE BLUE SCHOONER

Like a blue island seen from a distance, gradually she gained shape and contour, and, close at hand, revealed her original and intriguing lines – the elegant, strong silhouette I had seen before. She had the air of having crossed great distances calmly, and was marked with a beauty only time and travel can bring. Not an intimate friend, but a passion that had dogged me for a long time. The blue schooner, a two-masted sailing boat which turned up from time to time in Brazil, and which I never allowed to escape without a little flirtation.

Rapa Nui, Polynesian for Easter Island, a beautiful name for a blue boat with a locker full of stories. Built in aluminium, in Tarare, in France – the shipyard that launched dozens and dozens of famous boats and expeditions. The blue schooner, more than just an interesting sailing boat, was a machine for sea travel: safe, independent and well equipped. A boat built to sail any course. And to return. Even more, a polar boat, which at any time might end up by crossing high latitudes to sail on the ice. A boat with a body and soul. The boat of my dreams.

To get hold of the plans for *Rapa Nui* was the first step. After all, she already existed, and her virtues and vices were plain to see. When the boat returned it would be possible

3

to make a more detailed inspection. Even with no funds in sight and using aluminium as the building material, constructing a boat like *Rapa Nui* in Brazil didn't seem an impossible task. For sailing single-handed or with a small crew it seemed to make more sense to rig her as a cutter with a single mast, rather than as a two-masted schooner. Maybe painted red, to make the hull stand out against the white ice. Incredible how easy it is to make plans on a white sheet of paper. And how, however vague, some early lines turn out to be crucial later on. Or dangerous. Even more difficult to imagine where these lines would lead.

Rapa Nui would make only short visits to the Rio de Janeiro area. So I decided to become bolder and more efficient in order to learn her secrets. Little by little her owners, Patrick and Gabi, became good friends and ended up collaborating with my plan to build a boat very similar to theirs. The last time I'd seen them they were anchored off Cavaco Island, at Angra dos Reis, bidding farewell to Brazil. They were off to the Falkland Islands, South Georgia, and perhaps even to Antarctica, and were spending their last days in warm latitudes. The blue schooner, discretely anchored in the quiet waters of Ilha Grande Bay, ready to face the *roaring forties* and the giant waves of the south, was looking beautiful. There was in that boat a blend of anxiety and happiness characteristic of those who travel far, yet are certain of their return. It was a farewell for me too. I would probably not meet them again for some time, and I was busy solving problems on land. But I loved seeing them before they left.

'So long, *Rapa Nui*!'

Building boats is an infinitely greater and riskier adventure than sailing them to the ends of the earth. It is a sickness that sometimes leads to stormy seas. A French couple who lived in Paraty had been suffering from this disease for some time and it was amusing to compare our symptoms and the irreversible progress of the malady. Our plans were different. They were thinking of a traditional round-the-world cruise, sailing through the calmer, but more crowded latitudes, with no fixed date for their return. I dreamed of emptier places – the polar regions – and, more than just crossing sea routes, I dreamed of a passage through the four seasons of the year. Call it time travel perhaps. To experience the whole Antarctic winter from one summer to the next. That was my plan.

The contagion, however, is much the same. In no time plans, papers, designs, sketches and endless calculations become the reason for your existence. Engineers, draughtsmen, contacts and yet more contacts, time slipping through your fingers, until one day something inexplicable happens.

*   *   *

It was terribly cold in Punta Arenas and there wasn't a corner where I could hide from the wind. Alongside a huge tug, a small white-hulled sailing boat, the *Belle Étoile*, was trying to find some shelter from the windy Strait of Magellan. When I saw a head peeping out from the hatch, I waved quickly, rather awkwardly, and the head replied with a friendly gesture: 'Come on board, it's cold outside.' In seconds I jumped down into the little boat. What a party! Heater on, cosy, messy cabin, five Belgian mountaineers sailing down to Antarctica. What a coincidence! I was also heading down to the frozen continent, but flying in a Hercules at the invitation of the Brazilian Navy, to spend a season on board the *Barão de Teffé*, an oceanographic survey ship. I had been waiting three anxious, nerve-racking months for confirmation of the journey. The plans for the voyage, which had been prepared at least six months in advance, were quite rigid. I was restricted to a timetable that covered the period up to April of that year, 1986, when the ship would return to port in Santos. And what a shame! In the Antarctic the channels and anchorages used by ships and small craft are not the same, so it was very unlikely that I would meet up with the *Belle Étoile* down in Antarctica or have more time to talk to them – and see how a sailing boat behaves in those regions. Nevertheless it was a wonderful meeting, there on the dockside on a freezing afternoon. I told them of my plan to build a sailing boat to spend the winter in Antarctica and about the difficulties of building the perfect vessel in Brazil. My witty host replied: 'I hope that when we next meet, you will be throwing me the mooring rope of your new boat!' I ran ashore, through the wind, exhilarated. I had loved the visit, the good wishes and even the name of the little boat – *Belle Étoile*.

'My new boat,' I thought. 'That's a long way off.' But with the drawings for *Rapa Nui* now in hand, I had taken an important step towards constructing the hull. The boat was, at this stage, no more than a pile of aluminium plates waiting to be welded together. I hadn't the slightest idea when these would take shape or if they would ever become a real boat. But something had been telling me, ever since I had left Brazil, that I should stop waiting.

King George Island, where the Brazilian Antarctic base is situated, and Livingston Island, are the two largest in the sub-Antarctic South Shetland archipelago, and are mainly of volcanic origin. The climate is cold and oceanic, exposed to the low-pressure systems that sweep through the Drake Passage, a 650-mile stretch of ocean separating the tip of South America from the Antarctic Peninsula. Antarctica was first seen by human eyes from this archipelago, officially in 1819, by William Smith, an English captain, though possibly long before. Hunters of seals and sea-lions and then, in our century, whalers were frequent visitors. Today a large number of research bases have been set up in the archipelago by different countries. Fjords, glaciers and volcanic rock formations are found everywhere and, though the South Shetlands are the first group of islands one reaches heading south from Cape Horn, they are not much visited by small boats or sailing yachts. Sudden weather changes, difficult sea conditions and above all the drifting ice tend to force small craft away south to Antarctic continent itself. Apart from the volcanic crater of Deception Island, the last in the South Shetland group, sailing boats rarely approach the Antarctic Peninsula by way of these islands. Instead they prefer to head further south where a greater number of anchorages provide shelter from drifting ice. And the weather is better.

Some days later, having landed at Teniente Marsh, the Chilean base on King George Island which has the region's only proper airstrip, we transferred to the *Barão de Teffé*, which then made its way over to Admiralty Bay. The red ship, which had once been named *Tala-Dan* and had a long history of polar travel, entered Martel Cove, where the Brazilian base is situated, pushing aside little blocks of ice in a crystalline and mirror-like sea. In silence we listened to the sound of these bergy bits tapping the hull, and looked. The first sight of this ice world is impressive. I looked at the ship's prow, cutting the turquoise waters, and I looked at the peaks and glaciers all around. On the left appeared the green-painted prefabricated huts of the Ferraz base. Then, right in front, a small shape stood out. A boat. No! A sailing boat. A blue sailing boat with two masts, its name painted on the hull in great slanting letters – *Rapa Nui*.

There was not the slightest doubt, there was my beloved blue schooner. There, once again, beautifully anchored. Right in front of me.

She had arrived the day before, straight from South Georgia, struggling against head-winds and currents. Against all expectations.

'Hey, man. Have you come all this way to carry on flirting with my boat?' yelled Patrick, after he'd identified the suspicious-looking figure sitting in the first inflatable to approach *Rapa Nui*.

A reunion that just a short time ago would have been unimaginable. On board everything was still the same: the same crew, Patrick, Gabi, the little dog, the cat and also a guy from Rio, the good-humoured João, whom I'd met before in Angra. Suddenly the invitation came:

'Why not come with us?'

'What?!'

'Why not come with us, Amyr?'

A fiendish invitation, and far from a simple decision. To abandon everything and jump aboard the first sailing boat that turned up was hardly one of the most appealing ideas I could have come up with. Especially bearing in mind naval discipline and rules. But there was no time to explain. *Rapa Nui* wasn't just any boat and this definitely wasn't an ordinary occasion. They were leaving for Deception Island and I had to make up my mind quickly how to leave the ship. It was one of the most disagreeable things I've ever had to do. But it was also the best decision I've ever taken. When at last Captain Alencar authorised my transfer to *Rapa Nui*, there were just fifteen minutes to cram everything inside my rucksack and jump aboard the blue schooner.

A few hours after we left the Ferraz base, we began to pay the price of our undue haste. The beautiful, strong sailing yacht as reflected in the calm waters of Admiralty Bay, now seemed like a peanut shell struggling against huge waves. Surprised by a violent north-easterly storm, we went flying down the Bransfield Strait, which lies between the South Shetlands and the Antarctic Peninsula, at an absurd pace, surfing down high, short waves with almost no visibility. The sheets and halyards were covered in ice, which from time to time would drop in trough-shaped lumps on the deck.

In front, breaking waves mixed with pieces of ice much

larger than the boat. Huge white walls of water lifted behind us, while at our bows, almost under our noses, without warning, walls of ice appeared. My Antarctic baptism – and my worst storm. But also the last on this trip. The peanut shell completed its mission the following day and without a scratch squeezed through Neptune's Bellows, the narrow channel that leads to the interior of Deception Island. There was no time to feel fear, cold or even happiness. Dropping *Rapa Nui*'s anchor in Telephone Bay, inside the crater of the island, I could hardly believe I wasn't dreaming

In a funny way and some days south, the wishes of the Belgian aboard the *Belle Étoile* came true. When we tied up at the dock of Palmer Station, the American base on Anvers Island, I ran forward to grab the painter of the little white yacht which had just crossed the Drake Passage on the first leg of its Antarctic voyage and was coming alongside *Rapa Nui* – the *Belle Étoile* itself. Seeing me on a sailing boat and not on a ship, one of the Belgians, laughing, shouted:

'You were quick in getting your boat, mate!'

'It's not mine,' I replied. 'Not yet!'

For eighty-eight days, until disembarking at Santos, I lived on a very special boat, a boat to be discovered a little at a time, a boat that showed me distant and rare places and was the setting for the telling and retelling of endless stories, and a boat which, I decided, no matter what the cost, I would never again allow to escape.

Rapa Nui, inspiring machine, irresistible passion, had woken me up. Because one day it is necessary to shop dreaming, take the plans out of the drawers and, somehow, start.

2

BOATS WITH NO SEA

W e were three now, and destined for Brazil. João, after five months on board *Rapa Nui*, had got off at Ushuaia in Tierra del Fuego, the first town on the first civilised land we touched. There was no way he could maintain peaceful co-existence with Patrick and Gabi. Accidents of human intimacy, very common in boats or any type of confined space. Endless stories remained. Some funny – some filthy.

It was also a filthy day with heavy seas when Patrick switched off the automatic pilot and took the helm. Gabi and I put up the spinnaker, but our timing and execution were bad. There was a problem up at the prow with one of the sheets holding the spinnaker pole – the kicking strap – and the smallest mistake would bring the whole thing down. Unruly and uncontrolled, the huge coloured balloon-sail was dragging us down into the waves at great speed, making all the rigging shudder. Gabi stayed up at the prow and I ran to the stern to man the winch, nervous, without much experience of situations like this, and above all, without a safety harness on. I don't know exactly how it happened. A big, impudent wave hit the boat from behind. We surfed down it for some seconds and suddenly *Rapa Nui*'s twenty tons of blue aluminium went totally out of

control. The boat 'broached' between two waves, with a
violent blow to her sides. Masts, sails and all went down
on the water and I was thrown up into the air. To fall
into the sea from a yacht with its spinnaker up and even
the gentlest following wind is one of quickest ways to end
your career. On the high seas, it takes many minutes to get
the sails down, to come up wind and be ready to begin a
search. Amongst waves, a man in the water is only visible
for a few seconds in each minute, even close at hand and
in good visibility. One single minute's distance is fatal.

The weather wasn't at all good and it simply wasn't the
right moment to fall in the water. But there I was, flying
out of the boat on my back and plunging into the Atlantic
with boots, clothes and everything, some two metres from
Rapa Nui. Not possible! It couldn't be true. I turned over,
in panic, still under water and, before I could even put my
head above water, my hands touched *Rapa Nui*'s hull. I
touched and felt the boat moving quickly away. There
was nothing to hold on to, I could only feel the hull, my
salvation, sliding quickly out of reach.

How often had I read a particular story in a history of
French maritime law, but it was only at this moment that
I felt its full horror. To touch and yet be unable to grasp
the instrument of one's salvation. In the Mediterranean,
in 1974, four couples aboard a yacht, built by Baglietto,
had decided, in the middle of a calm sea, to stop and
have a swim. They all jumped into the water without
noticing that no one had remembered to let down the
ladder by which they could return. The boat was found
days later in the same flat calm, its hull scratched around
it by finger-nails and the bodies floating. All of them died
touching the boat, desperately trying to climb back aboard.
At the inquest which followed accusations went flying in all
directions: the finger was pointed at the first one to jump,
and at the last one who failed to let down the ladder,
at the skipper who had allowed this to happen, at the

boat-builders whose design didn't include a fixed ladder, at the legislation that did not require this . . . none of it mattered. In this fraction of a second I remembered the whole absurd episode. And I had nothing to hold on to.

Meanwhile, the wave that had knocked down *Rapa Nui* broke up and rose over the back of the boat. My right hand, as it slid along the hull under water, became tangled in something. It was the last chock on the stern. I was dragged out of the water, without my boots. With my left hand I seized the side of the boat and came bouncing, like a spring, back on to the deck. It was incredible, but for some seconds I had been gone and then somehow I had been grabbed – saved – by *Rapa Nui* herself! Patrick was still motionless with shock and disbelief. I was left with a bruised arm, bare feet and a debt difficult to ever repay.

From that day a new journey began. Still recovering from the shock and still with some 700 miles to sail before arriving in Santos, I buried myself in a thick book that Lucia, a dear friend from Palmer Station, had given me. It was about Ernest Shackleton and his second expedition to Antarctica, in 1908–9, when he tried to reach the South Pole. This time leading his own expedition and no longer under the command of the Royal Geographical Society's eternal candidate for the conquest of the Pole, Captain Robert F. Scott.

Setting out from Cape Royds on Ross Island, where he had established his base after an endless series of set-backs, Shackleton and three of his men walked for 128 days, from 29 October 1908 to 5 March 1909, right to the heart of the continent. At the beginning, in search of the pole; afterwards, to save their own lives. They discovered the route and the passage – the Beardmore glacier – to the immense 3,500-metre-high polar plateau. This route would be followed, three years later, by Scott. Just ninety-seven miles from the pole, Shackleton decided to turn back so as not to perish on the return journey. A desperate trek

of 1,477 miles through wholly unknown country, to lose
– by so little – the greatest dream of all explorers. The
most difficult of all decisions, to turn back, not to give
up, but to start again. To begin again. This charismatic
Irishman, not always well prepared, never achieved any
of his objectives as an explorer, yet never in his life did he
give up. He knew how to transform failure and disasters
into a story of optimism and success. He never lost one
single man under his command and never did he simply
follow routes that others pointed out to him.

The building of my new boat was under way, but
there was still time to change her. The idea of repeating
the design of *Rapa Nui*, a finished piece of marine
architecture, didn't please me. She was something out
of the ordinary, a formidable boat. She still had secrets
I hadn't yet explored, an infinity of technical solutions
and even some interesting mistakes that I didn't plan to
repeat. The rudder and automatic control system were
simplicity itself, while her solidity and shallow draught
were exactly what I was looking for. However, two masts
with separate controls for their sails were hardly ideal for
navigating single-handed. I thought both the deck layout
and the rigging could be improved. I also believed a closed
pilothouse with 360-degree visibility, a bunk and all the
instrumentation to hand, were absolutely essential for the
busier sea-lanes or for waters full of icebergs. Deeply
interested and involved with this blue sailing yacht, I
decided to accept a suggestion that had arisen during a
conversation with Patrick about the future, and become
Rapa Nui's owner once and for all.

I would have six months to solve this problem and
incorporate it into the plans for the boat I was building.
But these plans weren't the same now. I was determined
to travel alone, and *Rapa Nui* wasn't ideal for this. I
should re-think, from the beginning and in detail, the
problems of sailing single-handed. A new project. An

16

enormous upset to return tons of aluminium that had been especially manufactured by Alcan, and to reorder everything again: cancel orders, re-do calculations all over again, and raise double the funding . . . patience.

I didn't want to struggle against the elements, to defy the polar climate, to survive the dark and gloomy Antarctic winter. I was no longer impressed by dramatic stories of suffering, of near escapes or of journeys that end in fiasco. I had just escaped from one. Studying accounts of previous expeditions, adding the experience aboard *Rapa Nui* and talking to experienced sailors – like the incredible Jérôme and Sally Poncet, who had spent the winter of 1978–9 in Antarctica in their boat *Damien II* (which had been built at the same yard as *Rapa Nui*) and who had returned every year since then – it was clearly possible to have a beautiful voyage without a host of problems. But to achieve that one needed to be prepared. It was necessary to start again. I hadn't the slightest intention of setting out on an adventure, an uncertain journey, without being sure that I would reach the places I intended to reach, and without being certain if or when I would be back.

3

HAPPY SHIPS

Oh joy! The lights of Paraty! Paraty, Paraty, now you cannot escape me. Or I cannot escape. Now there's no way back.

I opened the visor of my helmet with difficulty. I was shivering from the cold, my teeth were rattling as I began my descent. In the dark, I had no idea whether I would be able to find a place to land in the town. Perhaps I should have landed on Fazenda beach, back in São Paulo state, but it was too late now. There wasn't enough fuel to go back. The coat, the same old red coat I had worn in other scrapes, tightly buttoned up at the neck rubbed against my chin every time I looked down in search of a road, headlights or a village in the darkness. What an idea! My God, what a crazy idea! Nose dripping and frozen tears running across my face, blown by the wind I could almost feel the warm up-draught from the bay as soon as I crossed the chain of hills dividing the two Brazilian states. The only problem was to find a place to land. Engine revving slowly, wing steady, I held the controls with one hand, the other hanging on to the seat.

Having taken off from the football field at the shipyard in Guarujá two hours before, I had only wanted to show a friend how to work this flying contraption, a Micro-lite glider.

Unable to land, I decided to carry on. Over Caraguatatuba the wind calmed down, I could have landed there, but, why not carry on, to Paraty?

At about 500 metres above the town, I decided to swing around and land in Fresca Street, just behind my house, where the telegraph poles and cables were set far apart. Three hundred metres. Going down, 200. Everything dark. The quay, all the small boats, and the lights on Cobra Island; no wind, very good, back to the quay. A pass over the defunct filling station, Fresca Street . . . then . . . TUM, TUM, TUM, the ground. Perfect landing. What a relief. I stopped at the door of Dona Maria's garage. I packed up the Micro-lite and, happy as can be, walked the fifty metres back to my house, my coat in my hand.

Next morning, very early, a Saturday, I couldn't resist. I set off again, before anyone started asking questions. I planned to fly back to São Paulo by way of the Cunha mountain range, which was clear of clouds. Icy sun up there, I flew over Jurumirim, banking over the dear little bay, taking photos with the camera in my pocket and then circling upward to gain altitude.

At 2,500 metres, high, very cold, little Paraty was left behind the mountain range. Until that point it would have been no problem to glide back down and land in the sea, if there had been any engine failure. From that point onward, crashing into the Quebra-Cangalha hills wouldn't be so amusing. It didn't matter. I was flying very high and the little beast at my back was buzzing away sturdily.

Stiff with cold, my fingers were frozen in spite of heavy gloves. I heard a monumental crack and then the motor stopped, leaving only the humming of the wind. Jesus Christ! It's not possible! Before I could understand what was happening, I saw an L-shaped gash being steadily opened up in the fabric of the right wing by a loose black cable. But from where? What was this cable? I let go of the controls, got out of the safety harness and turned around. The throttle cable had broken, become tangled in the propeller and had then begun to tear the wing open. Holding on to the seat frame, I tore off my gloves and threw them away. Below, in a void, mountains and farms were spinning in circles. I was going into a slow tail-spin. What should I do? Maybe try and find a place to land quickly. Or choose a tree to land on. No, there was no landing place, only thick forest. Better to try and get the cursed engine to work again. I still had some minutes before reaching the ground. I managed to tie a loop in the little bit of throttle cable that was left on the carburettor end. But where on earth to find another bit of cable, string or rope or anything to make an extension? Jesus Christ, the black penknife in my pocket, perhaps I could cut a strip of material off my trousers? Terrible seconds, fingers deadened with cold, I managed to open the penknife; but there was no time to cut the trousers up. Then I remembered the little camera with its black strap: that was it. I cut it off, made a loop at each end, tied it to the cable end on the carburettor and sat down. I grasped the controls. But the new cable was too short. Shit! The forest was getting nearer and nearer, there was turbulence and everything shook. The key-ring! The key-ring on my belt, with the pocket knife, a present from Hermann. I put the knife into the loop on the strap and the keys in my mouth and pulled with my teeth and the engine accelerated! Only 200 metres between me and the trees. Pulling away with my mouth full of keys I lifted over the mountains and gained enough height both to calm the turbulence and my nerves. An hour later I landed beautifully in the Paraíba valley, near a telephone box. As always, it was Hermann, my friend from our student days, who came to pick me up. We laughed a lot about this story which could have cost some major scratches, and days lost in the forest.

A beautiful fright. Saved by a penknife and camera strap. It's a good story.

An adventure? No. Compared to everything else happening at the same time, one couldn't call this little incident an adventure. The building of *Paratii* was going ahead at full steam, but the most important item, the mast, still didn't exist. Or, more precisely, it had existed for a year and a half, a supermast especially made by Proctor's in the United Kingdom. And it was exactly eighteen months that I had been desperately battling the bureaucratic obstacles preventing it from being imported. The real adventure was the attempt to get this mast imported by legal means, without the use of shady intermediaries, customs agents or 'fixers'. Fixers of all kinds: the legendary Brazilian institution without which life really is an adventure.

On the Monday, after my fright in the air, I finally received clearance to take away the bloody mast that had caused so many arguments. And technical discussions. I had wanted the mast to be made out of anodised black aluminium. This caused considerable upset. The anodising had to be done in Holland, creating transport problems and an inferno of conflicting advice. 'Why black? And must it be anodised anyway?' For one simple reason that I was not sure would work. But it was worth trying. During the one great storm on board *Rapa Nui* I had seen the masts covered in ice. This froze the sails in position, preventing them being raised or lowered – and worse, built up a large amount of weight – a danger to any yacht's stability. I thought that if the mast was a non-reflective colour, it would absorb heat – from the light – and prevent 'icing'. 'A solar mast,' I joked. All black. An idea whose effectiveness would be proven just once – but for that I was eternally grateful.

Adventures. Negão was the person who really knew something about escapades during this phase. He and his huge, ancient Mercedes truck were always being called upon to transport the emerging boat or pieces of my dream. It was Negão who collected the 21-metre-long

parcel from the No. 2 container terminal at Guarujá.
Not knowing it was a fragile item, the forklift-truck
drivers almost destroyed the mast with two high-speed
cranes. A year before I had had to transport the hull
from the boiler-makers' yard in Rio Grande da Serra in
São Paulo, across to the Dinieper shipyard in Osasco, it
was also Negão who was in charge of the night crossing
of the entire city of São Paulo on his ancient low-loader.
As the load was five metres high, five metres wide and
fifteen metres long, he'd had to dodge traffic-police posts
and low bridges, lift high-tension cables and traffic lights
out of the way, cross pavements or central reservations
while driving up roads the wrong way. It was the kind
of mind-boggling journey undertaken only by those who
transport elephants, giants or pieces of hydroelectric dam.
And, one other time, *Paratii*, already painted red, had to
negotiate another set of obstacles along the roads before
reaching the sea. Another 110 kilometres on the back of
Negão and his truck. A three-day trip when I didn't manage
to sleep at all.

Adventures and more adventures. The manufacturer
of the propeller, despite having been paid in advance,
managed to delay his delivery for three months. Ninety
days, each day coming up with a new and even more
original excuse than the last. The boat and an army of
impatient suppliers stood waiting for the screw to be
put on so she could be loaded up and tested before the
rapidly approaching day of departure. The boat in dry
dock, perched up on the launching ramp waiting for a
bloody propeller, which each day the supplier swore on
the soul of his mother was going be delivered. Until I lost
patience. Driven over to the factory in Hermann's Toyota
(I was too nervous to drive), carrying a well-sharpened
axe in one hand and my black penknife in the other, to
dispel any doubts about my intentions, I climbed on to the
receptionist's desk at the factory (which was called Hope)

and offered my point of view in a very well-educated and balanced way.

The propeller, magically and with great courtesy, appeared. Badly cast and unbalanced, but it appeared. As did dozens of other components or pieces of equipment that had been sent back, complained about, or otherwise been found wanting. Difficult work. We were struggling then to track down one single item that had suddenly vanished from Brazil because of supernatural phenomena related to the country's two macro-economic adjustment plans: quality workmanship.

There was a shortage of everything. And worse, products were being sold as if they were what they were not. Ordinary batteries for alkaline cells, 304-grade stainless steel as if it were 316-grade; electro-plated items as if they were solid, sell-by dates ignored, packaging damaged, spare parts non-existent. A tragedy. A true adventure.

There is a difference between journeys and adventures. Crossing the Atlantic, exploring the upper Amazon river or hurtling across the Drake Passage were definitely not adventures. Even crashing my Micro-lite up on the Quebra-Cangalha mountains and spending days hacking through the forest with just a penknife wouldn't have been an adventure because I would have had a compass and a place to go. A bearing and a destination make all the difference to any situation. Especially at sea.

I love travelling, very deeply. I know that journeys – not adventures – begin long before the date of departure, often in strange, funny or even unpleasant places. The *Paratii* voyage began long before my departure from Jurumirim, in fact at a round table-top with the signing of a contract in May 1986. This document – the source of ideas I was to develop – was the fruit of many adventures and more work than any single voyage could ever inspire. I had written it on board *Rapa Nui*, soon after the accident returning from Antarctica. In forty pages of a blue-covered notebook I had set out in detail what I planned to do, how I would do it and, finally, how much the whole affair would cost.

Sure enough, plans, projects, boats and voyages don't fall from the sky nor materialise by divine favour.

Almost all the next year was spent searching for financial resources to realise the plans in that blue notebook. I turned down an offer from one big company for reasons that seemed, at the time, incomprehensible. The company was prepared to invest in the project only so long as it was successful. It was prepared to sponsor the idea on a deep-background basis until it was certain there was no risk of the venture backfiring. Well, thank you very much. I needed real support, right from the beginning, from those who believed in every line written in that blue notebook: sponsors who would share in the risk. There is no human activity that does not involve some risk. There are even risks attached to sitting down quietly to read, if you are searching for something and have ideas in your head.

The biggest threat to the 'great journey' – difficult to explain – did not lie at sea but on land – on the drawing boards, in the quality of the components, in the care taken to assemble them, in the level of preparation and in the courage to make and remake everything until it reached the required standard. Perfection.

I said no to the 'deep background' sponsor and then almost regretted it. Almost. For months, with the few friends who knew what was in the blue notebook we argued about just how far it was worth going without making any concessions, how far one should insist. Patience, I thought. Even if it took me ten years, I would insist. It didn't take as long as that, but the months that followed went by almost as slowly.

Then a serious proposal came from a food company – Quaker Oats. Representing less than 5 per cent of the money needed for the project, to accept it seemed both daring and risky. But it was honest. 'We don't want anything in return, beyond sharing risks with you. We believe in your project and we hope it will succeed.'

Fair enough, I accepted. It was not a solution to any problems; quite the contrary, in fact – but it was a first step, a serious commitment from which I would have to construct the boat and the voyage.

It was also the kickstart that made me forget all the other prudent counsel I had received from experts on the subject. Before the end of 1986 I had decided to buy *Rapa Nui* and learn what I still needed to. My friend Cabinho, an experienced yacht designer, had already supplied the first set of plans for a new boat, exactly as I wanted. He worked with Furia, a naval architect, a man capable of the most impossible calculations whom I could call up at any hour of the day to alter my plans and argue with. I decided to put the actual building of the boat into the hands of Jean Dualibi, an architect, almost a brother, funny and good-natured, with no experience whatsoever of boat-building. He possessed, however, the one quality that is crucial to boat-building: congenital curiosity. He would have been able to build supersonic trains or spaceships if one were to hand. And we had *Rapa Nui* to hand. We set up a workshop for various experiments and a kind of team was born.

By the end of the year we had managed to arrange an appointment to explain the project to the Villares Group, a Brazilian steelmaking and industrial company, in the hope that they would be our main sponsor. I knew that half the board was against the idea and didn't expect a favourable result. But I urgently needed support; welding of the aluminium plates had already begun. There I was in the main building at the Villares Group explaining my project to eleven people who think, breathe and live steel. Philosophically and chemically, steel is the enemy of aluminium. I was careful not to over-use the word aluminium. I referred to it as a metal boat. Then came the final question from André Musetti, the only board member who had showed any sympathy for my project. 'What were the three other boats that have spent the winter in Antarctica made of?'

That's it, I thought, end of meeting. And I replied:

'Steel.'

'And what will you build your boat from?'

'Aluminium.'

This was the start of an endless argument over the advantages of steel against aluminium. I knew where it would end.

That's when they hit me with a dry, direct question.

'Can your boat be built of steel?'

'Yes. Just like most polar boats.'

'Would you build your boat out of steel if that was the condition for Villares to finance your voyage completely?'

I had been expecting this and the truth was that the boat certainly could have been built of steel. In fact, it would have made the job a great deal simpler.

'I'm sorry, but if my boat is to be built one day, it will be as described in the blue folder you received. In aluminium.'

The meeting ended, rather coolly. When I returned to my office it felt like a wake. Peter and another friend who had been at the meeting were ready to kill me.

'How could you? How? What difference would it have made to build the boat in steel, Amyr?'

The following morning, at the desk of Quartim, my bank manager and close friend, the telephone rang. Despite his 150-kilo bulk, Quartim managed to pass over the receiver.

'It's for you. The secretary of Paulo Villares, president of the company.'

Good God! I took the receiver. Paulo Villares came on the line. The project had been unanimously approved.

This was the first resistance test of my project: a steel

company had taken on board an idea that depended on aluminium, because what is important is the material the will is made of, not the boat.

The second resistance test occurred when Negão turned up with his rusty truck to take the boat from the shipyard to the slipway. Coming out of the shed, one of the cranes fell over and the boat careened down a steep slope. Apart from foul language and minor heart attacks, there was no damage done and the incident provided a practical demonstration that our chosen building technique – using thick aluminium sheets without stringers – was the right one.

Exactly on that day, as *Paratii* was being winched back upright again, I started to like the look of the boat and her calm, strong style. My only wish was that one day, when she was complete, she would also be a happy ship.

Difficult to define exactly what is a happy ship. It starts with some inner strength, but it also has to do with the spirit of those who work and live on her. Sailors, in the old days, used the term a lot. They'd say, though there is no such thing as an unhappy ship, there are some vessels that are clearly better, and on them, everything is in order and works.

*   *   *

Roald Amundsen went through the greatest test of his life in September 1909. Any long sea journey or polar expedition depends on the strength of the ship. Three years previously, in October 1906, the taciturn, slim Norwegian had sailed under San Francisco's Golden Gate, aboard the minuscule *Gjöa*, completing the 'insurmountable' northwest passage for the first time in history, sailing from the Baffin Sea to the Bering Strait. *Gjöa* had spent three years in the Arctic, and is still afloat today (I have a beautiful 1:50 scale replica model of her on my work-table). But she was, nevertheless, too small for his next project: to drift across the Arctic from the Bering Strait and so arrive at the North Pole. There was only one boat in the world for this task: the *Fram*.

That September Roald Amundsen made his way up into the Arctic Circle to visit the most famous polar explorer of all times, Fridtjof Nansen, who lived in an imposing house known as the tower of Polhogda. His mission was difficult: to ask Nansen to lend him the *Fram*, which was then and still is the most extraordinary polar ship ever built. It was in this ship that Nansen had completed his own polar drift. (I have 1:50 scale model of this boat too, which is even more beautiful than that of the *Gjöa*). A highly delicate mission also because Nansen still had plans for another attempt to reach the North Pole. Already married, he was also involved in important affairs of state in a newly independent Norway. *Fram* had been laid up. Ten years older than Amundsen and a cold, calculating personality, Nansen had once declared: 'Life has no meaning. There is nothing called meaning in nature. Meaning is a purely human concept which we've put into existence.' At the same time he was not wholly insensitive. He makes me think of the shepherd in Alberto Caeiro's book – one of Fernando Pessoa's alter egos.

To lend the boat would be, more than losing it, abdicating his life as an explorer.

Standing at the bottom of the steps leading up to Polhogda, Amundsen received a curt reply that was to change both men's lives: 'You shall have the *Fram*.' Nansen, then a minister of state, a former ambassador and a Nobel laureate of 1922, would never again return to the frozen north, regions his ship knew so well.

Two further events in the same month, September 1909, changed Amundsen's life and the entire history of polar exploration. All over the world newspapers were reporting the return of Amundsen's friend and old companion from an Antarctic voyage aboard the

Belgica, Dr Frederick Cook. He had reached the North Pole on 21 April 1908. Less than a week later, the *New York Times* ran a very different headline: 'Robert Peary reaches North Pole on 6 April 1909.' This started a quarrel which ended with Cook's unfair conviction and imprisonment, on the grounds that he had failed to produce sufficient navigational proof that he really had reached 90° north. Nansen's dream, now Amundsen's, had been doubly shattered. The young Norwegian made no alterations to his plans and, officially at least, carried on with his preparations for the North Pole. But, in total secrecy, he began to plan a radical alteration in his plans.

Again in September, this time on the 13th, *The Times* in London announced Robert F. Scott's expedition, which would attempt to reach the South Pole in the following year. A few months before the departure of both explorers, no one could have imagined that a race between two countries and two nations had begun in the head of a Norwegian who inverted his life's dream 180°, and with Napoleonic audacity, secretly shifted his objective from the North Pole to the South Pole. The last news the world was to hear from the *Fram* over the next two years was an enigmatic telegram that Amundsen sent to Scott: 'I'm going south. Amundsen.'

The difference between the English expedition and the Norwegian one was much like the difference between prose and poetry; only poetry can describe the voyage undertaken by the *Fram* and her crew.

Amundsen weighed anchor at midnight on 7 June 1910, slipping silently down the fjord of Christiania, later to be named Oslo, with no farewells. His crew still thought their destination was the Arctic, which they would reach via Cape Horn and the North Pacific. There were no crowds to send off the *Fram*, no celebrations or valedictory speeches invoking glory, courage and human bravery. Instead the little three-master – which also pioneered diesel propulsion at sea – left quietly and confidently, personifying the spirit of her commander and indeed that of the Norwegian people.

The *Terra Nova*'s send-off was a completely different affair. The farewell celebrations for this mighty British expedition to Antarctica began a fortnight before her final departure from Cardiff on 15 June of the same year. The *Terra Nova* had been granted the right to fly the White Ensign, a prerogative normally restricted to ships of the Royal Navy. Freshly painted in black, decked out with flags from stem to stern, she had drawn cheering crowds on her way down the river Thames. There had been speeches and newspaper headlines glorifying the might of the British Empire, and the courage and heroic spirit of this nation that ruled the waves.

It was the end of the brief Edwardian era. Edward VII had died a month before, around the time that Halley's Comet had appeared. A palpable air of decadence hung over the last three decades of the Empire, after the glorious years of the Victorian era. The publication of Darwin's *The Descent of Man* in 1871, the death of Dickens and the outbreak of the Franco-Prussian War, transferring power to Germany, were part of this decline. It was no coincidence that Nansen, Norway's first ambassador to the court of St James, quoted from Tennyson's 'Ulysses' when describing the achievements of his countryman Amundsen. It is a poem that captures the spirit of the old Empire:

We are not now that strength which in old days
Moved earth and heaven; that which we are, we are;
One equal temper of heroic hearts
Made weak by time and fate, but strong in will
To strive, to seek, to find, and not to yield.

Even before the race between the two began, its tragic end could have been foreseen. Scott had no idea of Amundsen's intentions, and it was only in Australia that he received the famous telegram, 'I'm going south. Amundsen.' The continent might still be unknown, but there was no doubt whatsoever of the need for both dogs and skis. The Norwegians, who were excellent skiers, had been certain of this since the turn of the century. Days before Scott's departure Nansen, Peary and even Shackleton had insisted on this. But Scott's tragic failure was brought about by his own arrogance, a British sense of superiority and his inability to attend to details or learn from the experience of others. The whole story is written down in his own diaries and those of his crew. In contrast, the *Fram*'s journey and Amundsen's final conquest of the pole were not only a masterpiece of talent, humility and planning, whose groundwork was laid by literally hundreds of careful steps. They made the finest poetry of human adventure I know of.

For the thousandth time I leafed through accounts of these expeditions. I had just read a beautiful book by one of the survivors of Scott's expedition, Apsley Cherry Garrard's *The Worst Journey in the World*. I was even more convinced of the futility of struggling for glory or flags. I was convinced of the importance of working seriously, simply and purely for the sake of travelling.

History has also tended to ignore one crucial difference: the Norwegian expedition was the undertaking of one man, not of an Empire. Amundsen had sunk himself up to his neck in debt to organise his voyage, but he was the absolute master of what he was doing; a passionate sailor and navigator before everything else. Like the great Yann in Pierre Loti's *Pêcheur d'islande*, who went fishing not for what he could catch but for the simple pleasure of being at sea. Amundsen was accused of being amateurish, but through his achievements, he became a legend for extreme professionalism.

Scott, on the other hand, commanded an expedition

which, aside from its scientific rationale, was sponsored by the Royal Geographical Society and the British government, and its true mission was to win back honour and glory for a maritime empire that was by then visibly in decline. Nor was Scott truly in charge of his own expedition. In terms of planning, logistics and command, he committed crass errors. As an officer in the Royal Navy he imposed a military discipline and command structure on the 65-strong crew of civilians and naval men. This took away that most crucial human driving force: motivation. The crew were not confident about their tasks and the ship suffered constant technical difficulties. *Terra Nova* was not a 'happy ship'.

When the nineteen men aboard the *Fram* made their last landfall at Madeira, they were told that they were no longer going to the North Pole, but to Antarctica in a race against the British in which their sole hope of victory lay in uniting behind a common dream with each man knowing his tasks exactly. In achieving this they turned the *Fram* into a happy ship.

Working for months on end on my new boat, living with long lists of problems, that day by day were gradually finding solutions, and learning, in practice, the secrets and details that every boat hides, I realised that in spite of being a long way off our objectives, *Paratii* would eventually get there. When the modified batteries were finally ready they fitted perfectly in the only space that had been left for them; when the mast – after so many adventures – went into its Norwegian öre coin footing with the precision of a Swiss watch and thereafter never shifted an inch – the same coin as the ones that lay under the masts of the *Fram* – and when, miraculously, Eduardo and I avoided sinking a little fishing boat on our first outing from Santos, I realised one day I would have a red boat in my hands. A happy one.

4

DEPARTURE

P atience, so much patience. Three years would pass before the birth of a red boat, rigged as a cutter, christened *Paratii* as she began a clumsy descent down the slipway in Guarujá. Alongside lay the impeccable blue *Rapa Nui*, a silent witness to all the bureaucratic brouhaha and technological tempests which had finally ended.

The launch was on 30 July 1989, a Friday – a day that superstitious people say is unlucky for launching boats or leaving harbour. I was so nervous I forgot to pass the bottle of champagne to my sister, Cabeluda, to break against the bows. No problem, I thought, and threw the bottle quickly against the hull. Among those few witnesses who were present was another interesting boat. By chance, on the previous day Patrick and Gabi had arrived from France aboard their new boat *Fanfarron*. She was tied up at the Hanseática shipyard, tucked away in the Santos canal, just a few metres from *Paratii* and *Rapa Nui*. It was a strange meeting, just like the one in Antarctica that had taken place three years before. Now the three boats seemed like accomplices.

During this time I had heard about so many boats that in all likelihood would never be launched in the sea.

So many! Forgotten dreams, fantasies left abandoned in shipyards, ideas never brought to fruition, or purely imaginary journeys. Now I was free of that nightmare. Touching the salt water for the first time, my red vessel gleamed in the sun. It was the concrete, or rather metallic, proof that you should never give up. That I had had to start again, to prevent my dream from becoming one of those ships with no sea.

At 5.30 a.m., on Sunday 31 December, 1989, the alarm on my watch went off. I'd been awake for hours, waiting for daylight. Thank heavens for that watch, I couldn't bear lying there any longer with a hammering heart and a dry mouth. I jumped out of bed and went up on deck. At the beach house in Jurumirim the lantern was still on, and so was the light on the mast of *Rapa Nui*, anchored a little way out from the bay. Everyone was sleeping. I sat on the stern, wet with dew, and was blowing on a cup of black coffee when Hermann appeared. We exchanged a quick 'Good morning'. That was all. Just like the old rowing days, when we were in training before an important competition: 'Silence in the boat' was the order, 'Save your strength for the water!' But this time I wasn't in training.

Nobody yet knew the date of my departure. I would decide over the next ten days, depending on wind and weather conditions. But in the small hours of that Saturday night, the last day of the year, I made up my mind. Somehow Hermann had suspected what was going on. The ties that held the mainsail were already loose, the engine was idling and the winch for retrieving the anchor was in gear. With the first rays of sunshine the sea became a red mirror reflecting the outline of the mountain that rose behind Jurumirim, while only the tallest of the coconut palms were illuminated by the sun as, little by little, it entered the bay.

A beautiful place, Jurumirim. A natural harbour enclosed by tropical forest with a little beach at its centre. Here, under the palm trees, is our beach house. I had planted the smallest of the palms when I was a kid. In the days when the land was still actively managed, the valley behind the beach and some of the hillsides were covered with banana trees. But when they built the new road between Rio de Janeiro and Santos, the coastal banana boats – with names like *Grajaú*, *Meu Brasil*, *Fluminense* – gradually disappeared as the lorries began to do their work. In Jurumirim the bananas disappeared too and the forest grew up again. There is no road to this place, only access by sea, either from the town of Paraty, heading away from the main beach, or from Paraty–Mirim (little Paraty), which is reached from the other side of the farm where it touches Meros Bay. There is no electricity either. The nights are lit by lanterns or fireflies.

The most beloved of my canoes – *Rosa* – lives there on the beach, under an old mango tree. I love Jurumirum deeply, yet for the first time I didn't want to be here. It's hard to leave somewhere that has for so long occupied such a place in your heart. I needed to leave – quickly – before the others woke up.

While jumping into the small canoe Hermann could see through the clear water that a cable was fouling *Paratii's* propeller. Quickly he dived and freed it. There was no time to thank him.

'Take care, Amyr.'

'Don't worry.'

That was all I managed to say as the canoe made its way back to the beach.

The truth was I had left long before. The final months had been hell. Thousands, millions of details; documents, decisions, problems both great and small all had had to be dealt with. Yet, as the last day approaches, we begin to depart. The months pass by, the tension increases, the last weeks, the last day, and then, finally, comes the real and actual moment of departure.

The noise of the anchor chain betrayed me as it came up. Eduardo saw me when I was at the mouth of the bay. He was yelling something I couldn't understand. After a few seconds I saw Cabeluda's blonde hair, as she waved from *Rapa Nui*. But I was already far away. Ufa! A huge lump in my throat. I didn't turn back to look any more. No goodbyes. Better that way.

I turned on the automatic pilot and put up the sails, first the main and then the two in front. Incredibly, everything seemed to be working. I went back to the chart table in the 'tower' (my raised pilothouse), opened up map No. 19 002, South Atlantic, and hurriedly, jotted down the hour of departure – 9:01 GMT – page one of my diary.

The calm sea, with a long and smooth swell, made the boat rock gently. I went to the prow to secure the heavy anchor properly. Perhaps I should have taken it to be stored in the hold until I came in sight of land again. It weighed fifty kilos in addition to the long and heavy anchor chain, but I decided to leave it in position in case of an emergency.

With my feet resting against the points of anchor and my legs against the pulpit, I settled myself at the extreme front end of the boat as though I were a carved bowsprit from the São Francisco river while *Paratii*, under full sail, automatically, silently, held her course.

A little before 11:00 GMT I passed Joatinga Point, 'Cape Horn'; then changed my heading to true south. This was not a short cruise. At last, open sea. To the east, Africa; to the south, my next stop, the Antarctic Peninsula.

Motionless in the bows, I kept watching the last trees still visible on the point as they steadily disappeared. Trees. Fifteen months to the next tree! It sounded like forever.

Curiously, though, it was neither the distance nor the time that made me nervous; it would be fifteen months before I saw another tree if everything went well, if I made no mistakes, if nothing on board broke down. At that moment, this was all I wished for. For boats are unpredictable creatures who sometimes like to make problems or to change course without much explanation. For once in my life I hoped not to see a single tree, at least not before the expected moment. To connect – with no stops – the coconut palms of Jurumirim to the glaciers of Antarctica which would be my companions until the next summer. It was for this that I had been preparing all these years and for this that I had taken such care in building *Paratii*.

Twice the day of departure had been delayed for a whole year. Two full years of delay – a shocking scandal – because I had decided not to make any concessions regarding the safety of the boat or the plan I had made. That meant being patient with the timetable. I had no wish to hurl myself into adventures or serious scrapes, especially in a region where the moods of the elements have a terrible reputation. After all, the two years had gone by and those wicked delays had been forgotten. And I was setting out just as I had dreamed. Armed to the teeth. And yet, my God, I was nervous. I knew I would encounter many more problems than you could ever dream up at a drawing board in the office, or sitting on the deck of a boat that has never left the tropics. During all those years of discussions, sketches and fresh starts, I had learned that the real danger to any plan lies in its details. Which details? That was the secret. I would find out soon enough. I left behind a crew of friends, suppliers and engineers who had been driven mad by those details. Things reached the point where, after work was over, they used to sit around joking about how to sink *Paratii*. Epidemics, tidal waves, insanity, metallic corrosion, *coups d'état*, the devil knows what. The funny thing is that many of the most interesting solutions and the cleverest details were the fruit of these sessions.

None of this mattered. I was nervous and tense. I had never been in sole charge of a boat the size of this one. Twenty-five ton, a 21-metre mast, three and a half years of complete autonomy on board. A red vessel advancing ceaselessly, day and night, southward.

I remained up in the pulpit at the bows, admiring the progress of this strange sailing machine, which would also be my home for several summers and winters. I was by no means certain that I would be able to make her follow all the dotted lines marked on my charts. Yet I was now certain that there was absolutely no reason why I should not.

The offshore breeze changed into a modest wind. *Paratii* heeled over a little and seemed to become more comfortable. I went below decks to check out a strange noise I could hear coming from the heads in the bows. The door of the medicine cabinet had opened and was banging madly against the wall. I closed it and when I went out I was surprised to find there was no longer any sign of land. Nothing but sea. Not even some dolphins to wish me a good journey. My horizon was now 360° and would remain that way until an island, a continent or at least an iceberg should appear. An immense horizon, but temporary. I had calculated the crossing to Antarctica would take twenty-nine days, and as there was only open sea until I got there, it was just a question of time before this horizon would be broken. And work.

Mysteriously, my nervousness vanished. It was as though a menacing coastline had disappeared. Sitting at the boat's 'focal point' with my back against the mast, holding a cup in my hands and chewing a piece of chocolate, was the most relaxing thing in the world. Gazing at my own private horizon, mouth full, celebrating my greatest achievement – having departed. I had set out on my longest journey ever, and even if it were to last just one miserable day, I had at least escaped from the greatest peril for any voyage: not to leave at all.

I wasn't setting sail on an endless journey, to wander on an abandoned, directionless *Mary Celeste*, at the mercy of the winds and the tides. I had an exact destination to reach and a fixed length of time to stay there, although I knew that my voyage would only end when I set foot again on the piece of sand I had just left. Weird: the object of my journey was just a single day behind me, and yet it would be a year and a half before I got back to it again. How I would miss it!

The sun touched the horizon at 6.15 p.m., Brazilian time. I glanced quickly at the sails, set the alarm clock and settled down in my bed for 45-minute nap. I fell asleep happy and contented, thinking of the place twice as far away as Antarctica – Jurumirim. Because, basically, I had set sail in order to return.

5

IN THE LAND
OF THE ALBATROSS

Within seconds the tiny white spot hidden in the wave became a shape and, ZAP, shot straight past me. It was a light – a drifting electric light bulb! What pleasure to pick up an ordinary light 200 miles off the coast on the morning of the very first day of the year. In spite of my tiredness, there was a fantastically good mood on board. I knew that getting used to the business of waking up every forty-five minutes would take some time; but there was no other way – that's how life must be organised when you sail single-handed. Every forty-five minutes, at first with the help of a shocking alarm clock, I had to to get up, quickly check the instruments, the sails and the horizon, look out for unwelcome ships and then, get back to the pillow for another nap. The big difference was that on *Paratii* I could do all this without having to put on boots and coat to go on deck with my hair flying in the wind. I didn't even need to get out of bed. I wasn't sleeping inside the boat in a normal cabin, but in a specially designed bunk installed in the pilothouse with its seven panoramic windows and main hatch to the side. It even had a skylight for looking at the stars – the invention of a film-maker friend, Zetas, who had paid a visit while *Paratii* was being built.

'What are you going to do up there in that little space?'

'Oh, I don't know. Watch the sea, I suppose,' I answered.

'Why not put a pilot's bunk in there with a view of the sea?'

Done. My adjustable, panoramic and fold-away pipe berth was born. 'Here, in the realm of blind ships, he who sleeps with one eye open is a king who also sleeps in peace,' I thought, my nose glued to the window, waiting for the alarm to ring.

Nothing could escape my eye – not the drifting bulb, not one of the halyards on the mast, which came loose and could have made a serious mess, not even a passing ship. Humming one of those horrible tunes that get stuck in your head, I jumped out of bed to make breakfast. I had no New Year's resolutions, no important projects or plans for the future; nothing. There was no celebration, and I was happy. During New Year's Eve, the only notable event had been a ship on a threatening course, which appeared three minutes before midnight. I cleared it without problems, and put the boat back in command of my 'slave' – the automatic pilot – and put my head down for another forty-five minutes of dreams and distant thoughts soon to be forgotten.

On the Tuesday, the second day, a determined south-easterly breeze set in after some periods of calm, and I logged another 201 miles southward. Not bad. *Paratii* was laden to the gunwales, with not an inch of spare space, but she was going like a bomb. During the weeks being loaded up at the Hanseática dockyard, as each item was stowed she would settle a little deeper into the water and my heartstrings would be pulled a little tighter. Some of the items in the inventory were worrying: three cubic metres of heating fuel; one and a half tons of food; 500 kilos of books; almost two kilometres of assorted cable and rope; sledges; inflatable boats; cubic-volume calculations; instructions for spare parts; charts – a nightmare. It was a never-ending operation, miraculously successful. Everything stowed away in its place. And even with so much ballast, we were sailing beautifully.

I decided to celebrate with an elaborate lunch, before we started to meet head-winds. But the party almost ended in disaster.

The galley had been designed to work at any angle. Even with the boat heeled over, there was always a place to hold on to with one hand, while keeping the other free to deal with pots and pans. With my back braced against the wall and my knee wedged against the work-top, I couldn't find the automatic lighter, which must have flown into some corner. I opened one of the drawers looking for matches and at the moment of striking, I noticed a strange smell. 'Jesus Christ! Gas!'

For various reasons, I had opted for gas for cooking, knowing that one has to be doubly careful when using it in boats. Because of its density, leaked gas accumulates in the hold and simply won't go away. Distractedly happy during my last night-time attack on the kitchen, I'd left all the taps in the vertical position, as I always did at home or aboard *Rapa Nui*. But on the new stove fitted on *Paratii*, the 'off' position was horizontal. Even worse, I hadn't turned off the main valve as one always should. Because of my carelessness, the hold had filled up with gas during the night, so if I had struck a match my long journey would have ended with me flying spectacularly in little pieces along the coast of Santa Catarina state. This carelessness could have cost me everything. I lost my party spirits, my appetite, and spent two hours pumping gas out of the boat, determined in future not to blow myself to bits.

Oddly, there are many more dangers inside a boat than are to be found on the stormiest sea: domestic accidents, a badly tied knot, an open tap or an over-hasty decision. Out there is nothing but sea: waves and wind, and they are not always bad-tempered. Sometimes there are great mammals or other animals living in perfect harmony. I remembered the hardened Argentine, whom I had met in the shipyard, who had worked on the *Legh II* (the boat belonging to the incredible Vito Dumas, which became the first sailing boat to circumnavigate the world through different latitudes). The Argentine believed that at sea there is no such a thing as big or small, and that all problems are equal. He said that if some are more dangerous, it's always the most banal, the ones you don't pay attention to.

During a quick appearance of the sun around midday, I managed a sighting with my old sextant to calculate my latitude, to check the instrument and blow the dust off my navigation skills. 26° 18′ latitude south, not too far from the position I had obtained in a few seconds using the portable GPS – a small electronic marvel that normally lived on the chart table.

I planned to continue heading due south, away from the continental shelf, where the depth falls quickly away from 200 to 3,000 metres, keeping a comfortable distance from the South American coast until the Falkland Islands. Then I would set course back toward the extreme southern tip of South America in order to cross the icy Drake Passage. Meanwhile, these names sounded very far away. 'If all goes well, we'll get there eventually,' I thought. But I didn't think too much about the future, busy with a host of little jobs between periods of sleep, and still enjoying being half-naked in the tropical temperatures.

On 11 January, with a south-westerly blowing and an unfriendly sea, I decided to give my 'slave' a few days off and substitute for it the wind vane which controlled a mechanical guidance system. An enchanting piece of engineering, delicate yet precise, it sets a course by following the angle of the wind, adjusting the main

TRUE BOATS ARE NOT
BORN BY ACCIDENT

A stack of plates and ideas that, once
welded together, begin taking on colour
and form until the day they set sail.

After the storm, the first
iceberg and the safety of
Deception's craters (*above*).
Rapa Nui, a boat destined to keep on
returning (*left*).

While disembarking from the *Barão
de Teffé*, an unimaginable encounter.
'Hey you, have you come all this way
just to flirt with my boat?'

In Penola Creek – sublime anchorage of the 'Argentinian Islands' – the wishes of *Belle Étoile*, as she lay alongside, come true (*opposite page top*).
The blue schooner, sailing towards Cape Horn, leaves behind humpback whales in the Gerlache Strait (*above*).

The leopard-seal,
Hydrurga leptonix, nimble
predator of careless
penguins, is even interested
in inflatable boats.

Clean socks and the
inflatable boat protected from
nibblers – domestic
precautions.

During winter, marking the passage of time.

A mess carefully monitored by a computer . . .

. . . while the freshwater-making equipment and the vegetable garden flourish in a cosy and warm environment.

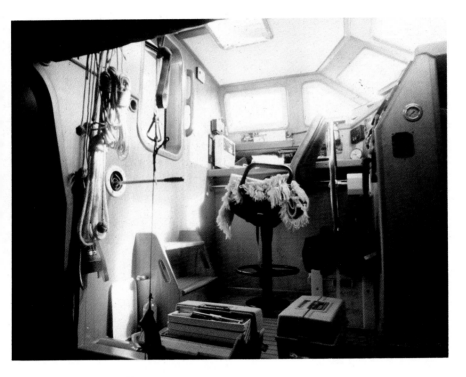

In this cockpit, well-lit for
hatching plans, the 20,000 mile
detour was conceived.

The navigation table and radio,
together with a lamp, which
during the dark months, never
went out.

Preferred location of night
attacks, the galley was never an
example of orderliness.

'Pancake ice' presages ▶
the big freeze (*over*).

rudder by means of a servo-assisted pendulum set right behind it. It's rather complicated to describe, but very attractive to watch in operation. I don't know why, but the device had been given the name Florence; perhaps something to do with her elegance and sensitivity. By never losing control, whether in heavy seas or in a flat calm, the device brought me great delight. Nor would it ever fall victim to the zigzag syndrome, as some human helmsmen do. Automatic pilots and wind vanes are the keys to single-handed navigation over great distances and I was happy, in spite of the head-winds, to leave the work to them. The great pleasure in sailing single-handed is to stay far away from the tiller. How pointless to spend hours at the helm, blindly following the compass needle. No way. What enchanted me was to plan the course, deciding on routes and directions that I would then suggest to the boat, while I went about my own business, watching the sea, walking on deck, or just thinking.

As it grew dark we were still sailing fast. At last the wind turned to the north, so *Paratii* was now speeding down the waves instead of sailing into them. At the tiller Florence held our course, while I reduced the area of mainsail by a fifth. With the moon not yet up, the breaking waves and our white wake made a wonderful light show. An impressive phosphorescence. Sitting out on deck I could see great greenish areas around me, forming glowing patches in all directions. When the full moon came up, the greenish phosphorescence disappeared, leaving in its place reflections of the moonlight. This was my first night of full moon under clear skies. To make the most of this night light, I inaugurated my fluorescent red coat intended for use in heavy weather, with its own built-in safety harness. With a quick manoeuvre, I brought in a bit more sail. But I stayed up on deck to make the most of the spectacle: a tormented sea challenging a peaceful, starry sky.

Only a few days before I would have been gasping at the prospect of surfing down waves this size. Now I was enjoying myself. Slowly I was gaining confidence in *Paratii*, making fewer mistakes when going about and even getting used to this huge and sometimes stormy expanse of back yard. I was living in a new habitat, one in permanent motion, and I was hardly aware of the fantastic speed with which the days flashed by. I was in international waters, Brazil left far behind, or rather above me, and the little bad moods of the weather and indecisive winds didn't bother me as they had before. I had caught up on my sleep, in snatches, so I decided not to go to bed until daybreak.

Rubbing hands between knees and with coat collar turned up to protect nose and ears against the cold wind, I remained motionless until I nearly leapt out of my skin. A huge, fast-moving shape hung in the air. At daybreak, right in front of me. A very special visitor.

The transition from subtropical and temperate zones to the sub-Antarctic zone is not simply a matter of crossing a line on a map. It's a transition from one world to another. Deep, clear, blue waters, poor in plankton and with few inhabitants become rich and dense and the oceanic landscape changes. Temperature, size of the waves, wind direction and the pace at which weather patterns change are some of the signs. But the clearest and most impressive sign of these changes is the growing presence of birds.

I had just crossed the 40th parallel, the latitude of the *roaring forties*. That set the navigation style required in these regions: with a north-north-westerly blowing at thirty-five knots. And I was being welcomed by the true master of this windy region, a wandering albatross, an adult bird, the most beautiful and regal being I had ever seen. In the past sailors thought it an accursed bird because it lives in these high latitudes between 30° and 60° south, in the belt of strong winds that circles Antarctica, laughing at storms with its charm and majesty; the stronger the wind the better. Its wingspan reaching up to three metres, it can live for more than seventy years. Four main species nest in the sub-Antarctic islands, laying one egg at a time. The chick is then cared for in the nest for 350 days, until April–May when it has grown enough feathers to survive its first winter.

My visitor, with his impeccable, precise flight, received me into his domain. Twice he flew around *Paratii* but, unusually, he was forced to flap his wings and then set himself clumsily down on the waves. His problems were just beginning: the wind suddenly dropped and he was forced to wait in the water like any lesser creature.

But as soon as I drew closer he took off, desperately running on top of the water until he could get up enough speed to get ahead of me again. Too proud to accept any of the biscuits I threw him. Turning in my direction, he simply glanced down at this strange red vehicle, incapable of flight, which was crossing his path. This encounter continued for many minutes until he decided to continue on his way. Many others came by afterwards, almost always on their own, sometimes hanging in the air so close to me that I almost believed it possible to touch them. Or to fly with them. But that was hardly necessary. I had been flying south since leaving Jurumirim, determined to land only when I caught sight of a small cove called Dorian Bay, beyond the domain of the wandering albatross.

6

RED ICE

PAPA – YANKEE – TWO – KILO – ALPHA-QUEBEC
PAPA – YANKEE – TWO – KILO – ALPHA – QUEBEC
PAPA – YANKEE – TWO – KILO – ALPHA – QUEBEC –
MARITIME STATION
THIS IS . . . PA/PA–YANKEE–TWO–A/ME/RI/CA–RO/MA
– SAN/TI/A/GO/SAO PAU/LO – TUNING IN ON TIME
ARE YOU THERE, AMYR?

Opa! There's Alvaro calling from São Paulo, right on
time as usual. Leaping out of my swivel chair by the chart
table, I rushed to take the latest barometer and temperature
readings. In my hand a sheet of paper with the readings
jotted down and a propelling pencil between my teeth. Oh
my God! I'd forgotten to adjust the antenna for the new
radio frequency. 'Just a second, Alvaro, just hold on . . .'
I fiddled with the radio, retuned it and we were ready for
another radio contact. I was always nervous during these
sessions, but Alvaro knew this and was patient with me.
With Brazil already far away, we were now talking on the
fifteen-metre band. I had left the Falklands to the east and
my route lay towards Staten Island at the south-eastern tip
of the American continent.

During the last radio session four days previously, I

hadn't been sure whether to cross between the island and the continent, through the Le Maire sound, or whether to take a course to the outside of the island. As a safety measure, I had asked for extra information from the Argentine tide tables.

I had already been through this channel on board *Rapa Nui*, when we'd anchored for a week in the paradisiacal Tethis Bay, on the far side of Staten Island, eating mussels until we almost burst. But sailing through the channel could be very treacherous. Of course the distance is shorter for anyone going to Ushuaia or the Pacific Ocean, but getting through the Le Maire can be a problem if your timing is not just right. Depending on the tides, there are five- to seven-knot currents running in either direction, visibility is poor and the long list of shipwrecks here is hardly encouraging. When the tide turns and the current runs against the wind, you feel as though you are sailing through a huge swirling cauldron of bubbling water.

Alvaro read me the tide charts, but I had already decided to go round, leaving Staten Island to the west. I wasn't dying either to eat shellfish or to see land. The chart position I had sent over on the radio already put me very near land, and my main concern was to stay well clear of the island. It's strange how, when you are at sea, just being close to land takes away a sense of peace. You lose something of the freedom that comes with the open sea, of being able to take whatever course you please.

Despite its fame and the deeds of so many sailors who have rounded it, the region around Cape Horn is a fascinating one. Anyone exploring the channels of Patagonia and the islands of the Cape will find an infinity of stunningly beautiful anchorages.

The flow of ships sailing between the Atlantic and the Pacific by way of Cape Horn fell drastically after the opening of the Panama Canal in 1914. Small sailing boats or Argentine and Chilean fishing vessels are seen nowadays more often than ships. The extraordinary number of shipwrecks and loss of life between Cape Horn and Staten Island came at a particular time toward the end of the era of sail. This was just before the opening of the Panama Canal, when the last of the clippers – often unfit to sail and under-crewed – were well into their decadent phase, but were still desperately trying to compete with the new steam cargo ships. As the prevailing winds and currents run from west to east, voyages from the Atlantic to the Pacific by way of the Cape had to be done 'the hard way' and were peppered with terrible struggles against the huge waves of the Drake Passage while the snowy, furious westerlies blew. Many ships found that, after weeks of trying to get round, they had to abandon the attempt and reach the Pacific by going the whole way around the world via the Cape of Good Hope and Australia.

Going round the hard way – from east to west – is not so difficult in winter and if, instead of trying to round the Horn close to shore, the ship heads due south towards Antarctica, until it leaves the region of the albatross and finds the gentler easterly winds. It was this strategy, no doubt, that accidentally brought the first explorers to the frozen continent.

During the night of Monday 22 January, I crossed the latitude of Cape Horn – 55° 59' south – and entered the Drake Passage proper. But it was a strange sensation. I'd always believed that when the day to face the Drake and its terrible reputation finally arrived, my teeth would be chattering and my fists clenched. Those blasted books always exaggerate. I was feeling a bit cold, nothing more. I was a lot calmer than crossing Joatinga Point. On board everything was fine. But not by chance. A few days before, *Paratii* had been put through a rigorous administrative review during which I had taken the opportunity to reorganise all the stores and goods on board. It's always a boring chore, but the truth is that even large yachts do capsize and I wanted to sleep easily. Everything had been designed to withstand both heavy blows and being turned through 180°, from the battery shelf right down to the engine mountings. The problem was all the cargo, which couldn't move a millimetre.

Nothing, not even the smallest tin of cooking oil, had escaped being tied up, screwed down or wedged in. The only things on board that weren't tied down were myself and the book I was reading – for some reason a biography of Mendelssohn.

The albatrosses were visibly larger now and more daring in their aerobatics, missing the masthead by millimetres or vanishing for minutes on end in magnificent great swoops through the waves. The Drake Passage is their patch, for here the sea stretches around the globe without any obstacle. These are the only latitudes where it is possible to sail without ceasing, either eastward or westward, on the same parallel. There is no continent here, just an uninterrupted ring of wind and water around Antarctica. It is here, too, that one can complete the shortest and the most turbulent circumnavigation of the world. This was what James Cook almost achieved, during his second expedition in 1772–4 with the *Resolution* and the *Adventure*, without confirming the existence of *Terra Australis Incognita*. Nor was this feat achieved by Admiral Bellingshausen, who in 1819–20 in command of the *Vostok* and the *Mirny* vied with the American sealer Nathaniel Palmer and the Englishman Edward Bransfield for the honour of having seen the continent first. It was only in 1831 that the first concrete evidence was discovered of a gigantic continent to the south – rather than simply islands or icebergs. This was gathered by John Biscoe in his 150-ton brig, *Tula*.

The Drake Passage is the bottleneck in this otherwise uninterrupted ring around the planet; its effect is felt both in terms of the weather and the currents. It is here that numerous, rapidly moving low-pressure systems of the

Southern Ocean concentrate, and this explains the sudden and frequent changes in the weather.

To the frustration of the albatrosses – and to my complete surprise – I found myself stuck in a flat calm before my second day in the Drake Passage had even begun.

Not a breath of wind, the sea was glassy and flocks of disturbed albatrosses were bobbing about like ducks. Less than 100 miles from Cape Horn was not the best place to be stuck, motionless. There were still almost 390 miles to go before reaching the Antarctic Peninsula, a little too soon to turn on the engine. I wanted to save as much fuel as I could for heating during the next twelve months. The next day, the brutal calm continued. Nothing could be more irritating. Sails down. The Drake Passage looked more like Rio de Janeiro's greasy Lagoa de Freitas Lagoon. Finally, I could not resist, I turned on the engine and headed southward at full throttle. Absurd to spend a whole day stuck in the same place. The automatic pilot took control. I removed the submerged part of Florence and went to bed. This was a day for radio contact, but during our last talk, I had already warned Alvaro that I would only send him a signal on reaching my destination. At 16:27 GMT, with eighteen long minutes before the alarm would buzz into action, I opened my eyes. I couldn't sleep, despite the hypnotic thudding of the engine. Still lying down, I noticed a mysterious object on the horizon. A flag perhaps, or a fisherman's buoy? What could it be? Oh my God . . . a sailing boat.

I leapt out of bed like a torpedo in search of my binoculars when I heard someone calling in French on Channel 16 of the VHF radio. What an amazing coincidence to meet another sailing boat in the middle of the Drake Passage! It was Eric, a very funny Swiss guy aboard his tiny yacht *Theoros*, with his girlfriend Martita, terribly seasick. We were both becalmed. We didn't come very close and, as they were moving much more slowly, I soon lost sight of them. We arranged to celebrate with a dinner of roast veal if we should ever meet again. What a party. Suddenly, appetite and good humour produced a revolution in the kitchen; soon a steaming *feijoada*, the Brazilian bean stew, with all its trimmings was served up on the chart table. Despite the calm weather, it was cold and damp on deck.

I had been dreaming of the first iceberg I'd see and knew the day was approaching. My only wish was that it wouldn't appear during one of my forty-five minutes of sleep. Advancing into the higher latitudes, the days were getting noticeably longer and it was dark for little more than a couple of hours. The engine had been running for eighteen hours before I was able to put up the sails again.

On Thursday morning, 25 January, the water temperature dropped suddenly, to almost 3°C, proving that I had reached the Antarctic Convergence, the invisible line that divides sub-Antarctic from truly Antarctic waters.

It was getting colder and colder – now down to 4°C – a rough sea and a 25-knot south-easterly wind. No one could call this a beautiful place, but at least I was progressing quickly. But when, when would I get a sight of land, of islands, of ice, of anything? With poor visibility and under a heavy sky, I couldn't stay calm anywhere on board. I put the chimney on the stove, lashed it on with rope to stop it being swept away if a wave swept over deck. But, for some reason, I didn't want to light the stove. It couldn't be far now: I had been heading down the line of longitude 64° west, and the last fix of position showed I had reached latitude 62° 53′ south. I prepared a soup of king crab and drank it, incandescently hot, standing by the window. The steam from my plate misted up the window and every few minutes I had to rub my gloves against the plexiglass to see out. How I missed the days of lunching on deck, stark naked. The cold was damp and penetrating; sky and sea were the same heavy grey. As I rubbed the side window to my left with a cloth, I received a shock. A blotch on the horizon striped black and pure white, in contrast to the heavy sky. An island! I put down my plate and the cloth and rushed outside. Jesus Christ a thousand times over! There really was an island on a bearing of 95°. Smith Island, perhaps. The time was 21:28 GMT, and at 21:42 I fixed a new position on chart number 3200. No doubt about it; no palm trees or beaches, only glaciers and snowy peaks. This is it!

I had chosen to approach the Antarctic peninsula by way of the tiny Melchior archipelago, 100 miles further south. Here, between Anvers Island and Brabant Island, lies the famous Gerlache Strait. From there on I would follow the Neumayer Channel, which lies between between Anvers and Wiencke Islands, and so reach little Dorian Bay.

A young Belgian officer, Adrien de Gerlache, had led the first expedition to explore these islands in 1897–9 aboard his three-masted ship *Belgica*. This ship was the first to survive an Antarctic winter, a circumstance prompted probably by design rather than by accident. Among others on board ship who gave their names to islands that I would soon be sighting – Danco, Wiencke and Arctowski – were the two young men who would change the future of polar exploration: Frederick Cook and Roald Amundsen. The book describing this expedition, a rare 1902 edition prepared on board the *Belgica* – which for years I had hunted in antique shops and book dealers – now lay open on top of chart 3200.

At 18:01 GMT on the following day, the same anchor I had hoisted up just twenty-six days before in Jurumirim, touched the bottom of the translucent Dorian Bay. As it sank through the water, the heavy chain still showed traces of mud that had journeyed 2,700 miles, to dissolve in that inviting, crystal-clear water. The heavy curtain of the Drake Passage had been lifted. Blue sky, no wind, an aphrodisiac sun. With a little patience and a few first scratches on the hull, leaving behind signature splashes of *Paratii's* red paint – the Neumayer Channel was nearly closed with brash ice – I anchored beautifully. As I'd dreamed. In peace.

7

SQUARE-EYED

T here was a fantastic racket around as I filled up the inflatable boat, using a foot-pump. At each pump of the bellows came a chorus of screams and gargles, a real circus. How wonderful to hear these new sounds after weeks at sea. The sounds of life. Not that at sea everything is silent: on the contrary. The sea is noisy, the wind more so, while the boat groans, cracks and growls. And little by little you develop an amazing capacity for identifying these noises; some slack in the rudder shaft, too much tension in one of the sheets or the nylon hinges of the hatchway; small objects that have got loose in the most unlikely places, and the dull thud of oil moving down in the fuel tanks – a weird symphony, where an odd note can mean a new problem. All this meant nothing to the gentoo penguins who filled little Dorian Bay. Their screams were like happy music, interrupted from time to time by high-volume gossip. But before paying them an official visit, I had to finish inflating the boat and fasten at least three long cables to the shore. I chose some small pieces of chain to wrap around the rocks, as well as some tubing through which to thread the ropes to prevent them chafing against the stone. You never know: in this region periods of calm never last long, and I wanted the boat to be absolutely secure in case a hurricane arrived. I lit the small heater after adjusting it, because the low temperature had made the diesel in the storage tanks become much denser. And only then I jumped into the inflatable when the little blue and yellow flame could be seen through the heater's inspection window, spreading its warmth though the boat.

Carrying chains, tubes and hundreds of metres of heavy rope, I set off, rowing the little boat on its first Antarctic journey. It took hours of searching to find three firm rocks close to the water-line, and to create the spider's web that was to secure *Paratii*. Underneath the snow there were certainly better rocks, but I'd have to wait until a bit further into summer to know which ones. I felt proud of myself after finishing this operation, and while climbing up the stony slopes surrounding the bay I stamped on the dry snow, to hear the squeaking noise of my boots as they sank in. I sat down on the highest stone I could find, from where one could see the strange red boat that had just arrived. *Terra firma*, yes sir! Firm as a rock.

The gossiping inhabitants of Dorian Bay didn't seem to be troubled by my presence. It was warm, or rather it felt warm, away from the wind in the hot sunshine. So I took off my boots and put my socks to dry on a nearby stone. Barefoot, I stretched out my toes, threw off my jacket and lay down in the sun wearing just a shirt.

Thinking back: it had been a wonderful journey. Having endured five low-pressure systems in twenty-six days, I hadn't been handed any special favours by the weather. But the fact was I just hadn't had any serious set-backs or been in distress; there had been no chaotic battles with torn sails or icy duckings on deck. And here at journey's end, I had made a peaceful and precise arrival. Perhaps getting the boat ready for the icing-over of the bay wouldn't be quite so simple, but at least I knew now that the riskiest part of the journey was over. The next stage would come only in a year's time when *Paratii* freed herself from the ice and began the homeward journey. But that would be another story altogether. Simply to arrive in Antarctica, safe and sound, had been the trickiest step, and represented more than half of the fulfilment of my plan. If during the crossing I had suffered a bad fall in the boat or any other accident, then the journey would have been over. Now I had all the time in the world to solve any special problems that might appear. A whole winter to do exactly as I pleased. Or as much as I could.

I pushed the little boat back into the water, under the watchful eyes of two penguins, who tilted their heads so as not to lose the tiniest detail of this strange object. Rowing slowly, I made my way back across the seventy or so metres that separated me from my home.

Paratii felt funny now that she was stable again, without the constant movement that I had become used to. No longer did you have to hang on to some support all the time in order to get from one place to another, or to feel you were walking up the walls. The strangest sensation was to sit at the chart table and realise that the coffee cup didn't need to be wedged in beside the radar unit, and that the bowl of muesli and milk was not going to suddenly take off without any warning, or that my pencil wasn't going to hide itself behind the main radio every time the boat heeled over to port. Seeing glaciers and snow-covered peaks from the same windows through which I had seen the Jurumirim forest and mountains, and instead of hearing dogs barking on the beach there, hearing the arguments of penguins in the snow.

Distracted as I gazed around, enjoying every single second of the indescribable pleasure that comes from arriving at one's destination, I almost had a heart attack when the alarm clock went off. 'Free at last from these forty-five-minute watches!' I screamed, hiding the alarm clock in the bottom drawer of the map table. Sleepy, but not really tired, I decided to go to bed before eating anything. No more did I have to lie down in the pilot house, but down in the cabin, in a proper bed, for the sleep I really deserved.

I dreamed of hammers, thousands of hammers tapping against the hull, accompanied by the sound of something being fried in a pan. What the devil was going on? I woke up in the middle of the night and putting my head outside couldn't see the sea, just a huge carpet of ice fragments scraping against each other, and against *Paratii*'s hull. Brash ice drifting in from the Neumayer Channel stretched as far as one could see. Broken, coloured pieces, some transparent and blueish in colour, others more of a milky, opaque white. Still well before sunrise, it seemed as clear as though the sun was just rising. Then the sun came up low in the sky, colouring the slopes of Wiencke Island close to my anchorage a golden red.

The temperature dropped quickly. I couldn't recognise *Paratii* at all. She had been decorated entirely in white: during that short night, tiny crystals had gathered on every exposed part. The sheets, stays, halyards, radio masts and even the wind generator's blades were covered with ice crystals, all facing in the same direction and all around five centimetres long. Now the sun's rays – though still timid – made thousands of tiny rainbows. I had never seen anything as beautiful in my life. There was no time even to pull on my boots; I sat outside admiring my gigantic Christmas tree, listening to the happy bubbling sound coming from the white 'field' floating on the water. The inflatable which had been left tied up at the stern, had been pushed upward by the ice and was asking to be pulled up on to the deck. Yet I was reluctant to touch the rope by which it was attached, and which ran down from the masthead, because I didn't want to damage its delicate crystals.

The camera! Oh my God! I had to rush for camera,

tripod and lenses. This equipment was shut up in a special case below, fixed to the saloon bulkhead. But then I thought better of it. What was all the hurry about? Why rush around desperately for 'daguerreotypes' I'd have plenty of time for later?

This was my first day in Antarctica and there were going to be at least another 390 of these before me, and who knows, many of them with much more spectacular phenomena to show me. What was spectacular was my mistake. It took me thirteen months to find out that the phenomenon of the crystals was not going to repeat itself, and that – like every other day of the Antarctic year and indeed like every other opportunity in this world – this day had been unique. It took me three months to learn that in the so-called white continent is to be found every single colour but plain white, and that this was at the same time a desert and a region of great vitality.

So I never took pictures of my crystalline Christmas tree. I just wrote down in my log the events of this first day on page nineteen, as item ten in the book.

From now on there would be a new page for each day. In these I would note down meteorological and climatic data, in the space that had been taken up with sailing and navigation details. In a second a week packed with so many events had gone by that I had to leaf through the pages of this 'memory' – the log – to know what I had done the day before.

The first radio contact with Brazil after my arrival turned out to be a party. Alvaro was anxious because of my week-long silence; Hermann was euphoric because of the way *Paratii* had handled herself during this maiden voyage. Dearest Cabeluda finally authorised me to open a box of Christmas presents that she and the staff in São Paulo had carefully placed on board, with instructions that they were to be opened when I arrived.

Loads of messages from friends, jokes, even a little

Christmas tree – for next Christmas, of course. There were presents for my birthday nine months hence and some letters to be opened month by month. Very funny all this; future news already in my hands.

I finished the radio link-up longing for a magnificent hot bath, but for that I needed to turn on the generator and sort out a small mistake I'd made during the crossing. Worried about salt water coming back through the generator's exhaust pipe if a freak wave were to strike *Paratii* from behind, I had sealed the outlet with a wooden bung that had swollen in the water and now didn't want to come out. Too much fussing. The exhaust pipe was right down in the stern and to get at that damned bung, I'd have to shift at least 500 kilos of stored food. Whilst I was about it I took the opportunity to reorganise the winter stores of food once and for all. That bath cost three days' work before I finally got into it. But, what a bath! A shave, a haircut and clean clothes. A revolution!

When I opened the skylight to let the steam out, I got a shock. A beautiful Dutch boat with dark sails was anchored some hundred metres from *Paratii*, right at the entrance to the little bay.

Aboard were Dick and Elly, an extraordinary couple with fantastic experience of the sea, whose path I was to cross again on the same latitude at the other end of the world. This happens so often in the boating world. I went across to say hello and was rewarded with an invitation to dinner. Superbly cooked fresh shrimps – I've no idea how they found them – washed down with an excellent Pouilly-Fuissé and a lot of talk. This first meeting caused me to bring forward plans I had been keeping for the future.

A couple of grandparents, they lived their lives in such a youthful, intense fashion that it was enough to inspire anyone to stop dreaming and take action. The *Jantine* was leaving in a couple of days for Europe, by way of the

Falklands and the Azores, so I took the opportunity of sending my correspondence with them. I also gave them a pair of oars, sculpted from a special wood called *guacá* with an adze and polished with shells and broken glass. Among all the primitive oars that I have seen, none can match the form and beauty of these. Beautiful, and extremely practical. Dick and Elly loved the gift. They left with the oars, half a dozen letters and kept on sending me news.

A few days after the *Jantine* had left, while on an excursion in the inflatable to Port Lockroy – a couple of miles to the south – I met Eric and Martita of the *Theoros*, the boat I had encountered in the middle of the Drake Passage. I'd seen plenty of tiny, ill-prepared boats around, but the *Theoros* took all the prizes. They had spent eight whole days trailing across the Drake, which is really tempting the devil. And now here they were, blithely anchored in the worst possible place, between sharp-toothed icebergs. Martita – who had never even been in a boat until two weeks previously – was clearly still in a state of shock after having saved both their lives shortly after our extraordinary meeting south of Cape Horn.

'Eric! Hey, Eric! Something is moving at the back!'

'Let me sleep, for God's sake!'

'But Eric! There really is something strange moving, come up here, come on!'

Unbelievably, even though they were in a flat calm, the rudder had broken and was literally hanging by a thread. If they'd lost it, they would in all probability now be resting in 1,500 fathoms of water. By sheer will-power some people achieve miracles – and keep their boats afloat.

That earlier promise of roast veal was beautifully fulfilled and for the next two weeks, sometimes with our boats tied up alongside, we laughed ourselves silly. Both Eric and his boat were radical. As well as a sailor, he was a philosopher and a rebel. Crew and boat fought night and day, but they made a funny trio.

Those 'mysterious forces that command the fury of the elements and the ferocity of the southern oceans' had certainly made an exception for the *Theoros*, which despite this being the worst season, managed to cross the Drake Passage back to Ushuaia without a scratch.

During the third week, these same mysterious forces showed themselves in Dorian Bay, just as I had suspected they would. While the hot sun lasted I had found an abundant source of fresh water and an ideal spot to set up my express laundry. A shallow pool of abundant fresh water lay between some dark rocks, which should remain unfrozen for a couple more months. I spent the whole morning working, shirt off, washing and rinsing out pyjamas, jackets and bags. By midday everything was dry and I was starting to gather up my laundry when the sun disappeared without any warning. The glass had been falling slowly and so I hadn't been too worried. But within half an hour what had been a soft breeze really started to blow and went on increasing steadily. The rocks to which I'd tied *Paratii* looked firm, but the trouble was that the boat was tied up facing north–south.

The wind, meanwhile, was coming in sideways on from the south-west and soon went round to the north-east in strong squally gusts. It was chaos: the ropes around the rocks were as taut as violin strings and the anchor chain screeched with every burst of wind. The problem wasn't so much the strength of the wind – it was blowing between 45 and 55 knots – but the sudden gusts. The boat would start to come up into the wind, the ropes would slacken, and then bang! another squall would strike and we'd be sent back toward the rocks. Nervous and unsure of what to do, I switched on the motor, to escape the rocks if one of the ropes parted. Now large, sharp-pointed pieces of ice – some weighing many tons – were coming into the bay and were getting tangled in the ropes. *Paratii*, secured by her bows, was hurling herself from one side to the other. The inflatable was tied up alongside, with the outboard ready for an emergency escape. I'd completely forgotten about it until, through the window, I saw a strange black object flying through the air upside down with a beautiful Yamaha engine and a red tank hanging off it. I rushed outside, grabbed this inflatable kite and rescued the engine and fuel tank, but, disaster, one of the precious oars from *Paratii* was lost!

The gigantic iceberg that some days before had run aground beyond the rocks, leaned over a little and simply burst into thousands of pieces, creating a wave that drew into the bay thousands more pieces of ice that had been trying to find their way past the rocks on the point. This brash ice now piled itself up at the back of the bay, so closing it off completely. Only then did the boat, now wedged between blocks of ice of all different sizes, finally calm down.

The wind blew until next morning, when, exhausted, I took my hand off the engine control and went to sleep. The temperature fell yet again, though the barometer was stable and a fine snow covered both deck and dark rocks around us.

From that day on I made a thorough check of the rocks to which the ropes were tied. The second largest of these, which I called the 'south rock' had been pulled loose by the gusting south-westerlies. The chain that tied around it had slipped down and the rope was loose. My God! What strength to pull free a rock of that size!

So a new plan for securing the boat was conceived and I planted a safety anchor on dry land, fixed due north-east of the bows, 150 metres away. It looked much better, but I would only feel really secure after the next storm, which, for sure, would not be long in coming.

Log entry for 20 February: 'Every good moment in

this place exacts its price.' And what a price. On the other hand when the bad weather goes every centimetre of sun or blue sky is well worth the price. On a dazzling and crystal-clear day I went back to Port Lockroy in the little boat. I almost succumbed to the temptation of a quick swim. Port Lockroy is a British base established in 1944, abandoned for many years. Now the penguins have invaded the two structures that remain standing. To the north of the main island is a small bay covered with whale bones of all sizes. In the past this was where whales were dragged up to be cut into pieces. In the whale cemetery are also to be found gentoo penguins, a colony of blue-eyed cormorants and the odd Weddell seal. This was my favourite place in the neighbourhood, somewhere I had thought of for my winter sojourn. It had two disadvantages: there was little protection from drifting icebergs and, because of the strong current running between the islands, the sea might take longer to freeze over properly in winter, or never do so.

I was impatient to see *Paratii* held fast in the ice once and for all, and to be free of all this worry of anchors, ropes and rocks. I couldn't imagine how, suddenly, the time would come.

During February – the first month – I became used to very long days and almost no darkness. I made the most of this time and got plenty of work done. I prepared two stores of food and winter clothes for use in Port Lockroy and Doumer Island during the winter. I set up a collection device for petroleum traces, which was part of a project on the breakdown of hydrocarbons which my friend Marcia from University of São Paulo was working on. I also repaired the two rubber boats, which were full of holes. The smaller boat, which was christened *Vagabundo*, had obviously been attacked by a seal or by a sea-lion, which I had failed to catch red-handed. The larger boat was giving problems at the points where its rubber material had been reinforced. In the cold these thicker parts became brittle and inflexible. Interesting that in the cold everything has an exact limit. And fragility can be more resistant than simple strength.

A weekly programme of radio contacts with Alvaro had been established, but always on different days of the week and with back-up times and radio frequencies in case we failed to link up. I retied the whole system of ropes and cables, and concluded that the idea of protecting those ropes tied around the rocks with plastic tubes, rather than using chains, was working perfectly. Learning how to tie up the boat is the number-one art in Antarctic sailing.

Using *Vagabundo*, I had invented a system of towing away any large and unwelcome pieces of ice that entered my domain and might upset *Paratii*. To fix the rope on to the lump of ice to be dragged away, I used a kind of ice screw used in mountaineering. Once again I rearranged my supplies of food, tools and spare parts. And, at last, I managed to communicate with the smaller heater. It was less efficient than the main one, a fantastic Danish heater, and also much more temperamental, but I decided that while the temperature permitted I would carry on using the small one because it had a little window that showed the flame. After a day's work it was a pleasure to sit down on the wooden bench in front of the yellow gleam of the small fire, with a good book on my knees, socks drying near the chimney and slices of cheese toasting on the small hotplate. The hours of darkness increased each day, as did the tasks left to be done. Fresh water and meals, maintenance of the engine and pumps, cleaning the heaters, recording data and collecting samples filled up a day in no time. Dozens of the longer trips I had planned had to be put off for the following year.

There were visitors, too. Every visit was a party. I met up with five of the eight sailing yachts that came down to Antarctica that year. The last of them was the *Oviri*, also being sailed single-handed, by Hugo, who had come down to spend the winter on Pleneau Island, near the British base of Faraday. I was keen to meet two of the bigger boats – one of which I met up with in Africa long ago – but they both abandoned their attempts.

More sizeable visitors, ships, would sometimes cast anchor near Casabianca Island in front of Dorian Bay. Researchers would come ashore in inflatables and be persuaded to carry my correspondence away with them.

Then came the smallest and most interesting visitors, indicating important changes on the Antarctic Peninsula. Weddell and crab-eater seals, a noisy sea-lion and flocks of penguins of different species. My neighbours, the baby gentoo-penguin chicks who inhabited the bay, growing bigger and fatter were more independent and would now fish on their own and, little by little, went off to lead their own lives. Another Antarctic species that appeared amongst the rocks was the Adélie, a small penguin with an entirely black head. They seemed to be the nosiest of the *Pygoscelis* species. I still wasn't sure if I would be enjoying their company over the winter, because most of these birds migrate northward, returning only the following summer. The exception is the majestic emperor penguin. In contrast to all other species, these lay a single egg on to the frozen sea ice right in the middle of winter. During the harshest period of the winter and without any nourishment, the male broods the single egg on top of his feet for the sixty days of incubation: alternating those most exposed to the wind from time to time. The females, meanwhile, travel north and return only when the chicks are born. Sadly, I was not to meet any emperor penguins. But the arrival of the comical Adélies was the signal that the sun would soon disappear for winter.

A small and energetic Adélie was investigating the anchor up in the bows and I couldn't resist. I had been told by Professor Villela, an old friend and veteran of

Antarctica, that the eyes of Adélie penguins had square pupils. A professor of Antarctic studies, physically he differs very little from a penguin himself. In his last radio contact a month before, he had mentioned this fact about the Adélies. In an attempt to confirm this, I grabbed the creature which was investigating my anchor and held on, despite protests and peckings. I wasn't completely convinced, but certainly its pupils weren't really very round. As soon as I let it go, it let out a squawk and calmly continued nibbling the anchor.

In March the temperature finally dropped below zero; every morning the deck was covered in snow and the rocks along the shore line were disappearing under a carpet of new snow. My laundry had dried out or rather, it froze completely, and each day water had to be made by thawing out the snow over the big heater. I had to exchange the small heater for this one, which sadly didn't have the little window and its glowing flame. Summer was bringing down its curtains. The last human visitor of the season was Peter Marquis, commander of Rothera Base in Marguerite Bay. With his team he had closed down the station and was heading off aboard the *Bransfield*, a British Antarctic Survey ship.

'Hope to see you alive next year!' said Pete, joking, as he gave me two tins of beer.

During the first week of April I witnessed a great exodus of my neighbours the gentoos, and on that Sunday morning, 8 April, *Paratii* was held fast in an uneven plate of glass. Dorian Bay had frozen over.

8

TIME TRAVELLERS

ONE DAY, IT IS NECESSARY TO STOP DREAMING AND, SOMEHOW, TO LEAVE

Theobald, the tenant who only spoke on the last day.

Not an imprisoned boat, ▶ but a time-traveller (*over*).

No longer a boat, but a red terrestrial station, held fast in the ice until the following summer.

I had just closed the deal for eight small calves and was loading them into the gaily painted cattle truck, when I saw there was a tempting amount of space left over for something I had long lusted after. An ox-cart from the Natividade da Serra region. Made of *ipé*, a Brazilian hardwood, with solid embossed wheels, the grain visible, it was perfect, to die for. In Paraty, a pair of buffaloes pulling the cart had been a great success bringing in the meat on the last day of the pentecostal celebrations.

Apart from the pleasure of riding across the town in such a unique vehicle, I discovered the secret of 'the singing in the wheels', that shrill and nostalgic melody made by the axles of these primitive carts as they lumber forward. Lard on the axles, a bit of coal dust and a wedge of *ingá* or some other green softwood, and you can produce a maddening screech. The music of wood on wood that could be heard long before the animals came in sight.

Certainly, *Paratii* now resembled an ox-cart, singing and yelling a strident song that sounded like anything in the world other than ice. A thick plate of ice held the hull. In the movement of the tide – that going up, would release the pressure, and, going down, would compress it more – one could hear the curious sound of the ox-cart.

Sometimes, however, the music produced by huge plates of ice pressing against each other, against the rocks or against *Paratii*, would be interrupted by a dull, metallic thud. More worrying: it was the rudder.

The slow movements of the ice sometimes caught the rudder in an uncomfortable position and forced it right over to the end of its arc, prompting a loud explosion.

Rudders are always the most vulnerable part of a boat designed to sail in ice, so *Paratii* was equipped with a rudder that would not have disgraced a nuclear-powered ice-breaker. Nearly indestructible it was, at the same time, extremely sensitive and efficient, as it needed to be for use with an automatic pilot. Designing the rudder alone had taken more time than is dedicated to the building of many a boat. Our task had been to reconcile two opposites: making it robust and solid, yet with a delicate action. Once it was complete, a desk-bound marine architect in Rio de Janeiro poured scorn on its indestructible and inimitable looks. 'Are you crazy?' he asked. 'Why on earth do you need such a big rudder? Do you imagine some Samson of the Antarctic plans to grab your boat by the rudder, shake it in the air and then hurl it against the rocks?'

That was precisely what I was expecting. And, just in case this powerful fellow decided not to let go of my rudder, I could easily remove it using a block and tackle mounted on a raised bar running over the stern, and designed especially for this job.

May turned out to be a musical month, and a hot one too: light winds whistled all the time without the thermometer dropping, which was a bad sign. It didn't take long to discover all the advantages of low temperatures – dry light snow, firm silent ice, very low humidity and absolutely no condensation. Any rise in temperature above minus 3°C was a catastrophe. Snow on the deck melted and then became ice, which forced its way into every nook and cranny imaginable. In the more humid conditions the mooring ropes became stiff as they froze; while on long walks, I couldn't sit down without getting my clothes soaked. A film of condensation formed inside the cabin and then froze on the windows and hatches. As the boat warmed up, this turned to dripping stalactites. Beautiful, but no fun. In this frozen world any heat actually makes you uncomfortably chilly.

Worse, on hot days tuneless soprano screeches added their voices to the usual ice chorus. Dorian Bay broke into tiny pieces that moved almost imperceptibly. The four mooring ropes attaching the boat to the rocks were constantly getting caught up on sheets of ice of differing sizes. I tried both to sink the ropes and then to raise them up so they would not be caught by the ice, without success. Stretched to their limits, at certain moments these ropes were subjected to terrible tension and cried out against the cleats. These cries, of course, nearly always started around midnight, just when I was fast asleep. Sleeping in the middle of a pop concert, I'd have to go out seven or eight times to slacken the tension on the ropes. And then BANG! The boat would come loose in its frozen bed and the rudder would spring into action. BANG and BANG again! From one side to the other. There were warm nights, though the glass was low and there was much wind. With the return of the cold the following day, peace was restored. With *Paratii* fast in the ice, a profound silence and well-being reigned: at least in the strange, moving world around me, where peace and silence took on meanings I had never suspected.

Silence was the vacuum between gales, when I could simply listen to my 'ox-cart' settling herself in the ice, or the sudden breathing of a seal coming up from beneath the bay, opening with its teeth a hole in the ice just metres away from *Paratii*. These breathing-holes, from which only a moustachio-ed snout and two eyes would protrude, had to be prevented from freezing over by constant nibbling. On a couple of occasions, quietly working outside, I almost died of fright when a high-pressure snort broke the surrounding silence.

The screeching of the neighbouring gentoos on windless afternoons was also part of my silence. There were now no more than 200 of them, but they seemed much more communicative. Waking in the mornings, before I had lit the stove or put the coffee on, as I cleared the new snow off the windows to let in more light, I'd yell at them till the veins stood out on my neck: 'Wake up, guys, the party's starting!' or 'Good morning, customers, the storm is over,' but pretty soon I degenerated into obscenities. Every day, more nonsense. And every day they gave as good as they got, answering back for hours as though auditioning for a voice test, heads up and flippers stuck out behind. In truth, I was the one who started it all by screaming some obscene rhymes when I was in the mood, just before going to bed. I had to stop under threat of hours of tuneless cackling in reply. Though there were few of them now, there were still some visiting Adélie penguins. I could distinguish them from the gentoos by their deep comical voices.

During this period of silence, I discovered a curious phenomenon. When the tide went out, the ice sheet was supported by what I called the 'south rock' – the fixing for two of *Paratii*'s mooring ropes. This left a space underneath the ice sheet which allowed me to examine the cables. As I prepared to enter this gap and crawl under the ice, my favourite black penknife fell down a crack. I let out a well-rounded curse and, to my immense surprise, heard the reply '. . . uck, . . . uck, . . . uck, . . .uck'. I swore again: '. . . astard, . . . astard, . . . astard, . . . astard.' Incredible; a four-way echo from four different directions, my own voice multiplied by four. When the novelty wore off, I binged on curses, funny words, and then the names of dear friends which I wanted to listen to many more than four times.

I then launched a rescue expedition into the space

between the wet rocks and the huge ice sheet above. Despite the discomfort, I managed both to retrieve my penknife and to examine the cables and chains, which, after months of tension, were in perfect condition. I spent the rest of the day fooling around with the echoes, making up new sounds or instruments, yelling like a loony and hearing my own voice four times over.

This was the day I had to contact Brazil for a long QSO radio session with Alvaro, and I found myself with almost no voice left to transmit the week's data. There were other voices filling up these rare silences. A weird guttural noise I could hear only when inside the boat. At first I thought it was the creaking of the mooring ropes. But I was wrong. It was my neighbour, the seal, swimming around under the boat.

Other voices were aerial. Only a handful of the many species of birds remained here at this time of year. There were the sheathbills, small, silent, daring scavengers, and the dominican gulls, excellent fliers filling the air with raucous cries and aerobatics. The skuas were aggressive, dark birds of prey that were always harassing the penguins or anything that encroached on their territory. By now the many types of petrel were probably migrating far to the north, while the terns with their pale bodies, red bills and black and white heads, were probably flying over Brazil on their ceaseless migration from one end of the planet to the other. They were on their way to the Arctic in search of the polar summer. I missed their racket at Port Lockroy or on Doumier Island and, in a way, envied their wanderers' life. So tiny, smaller than a dove, and such nomads.

The departure of these gypsies, as admirable as the wandering albatrosses, reminded me of a conversation I had had with the Dutch couple aboard the *Jantine*, during my first week in Antarctica. Like the terns, they were heading north, and this strengthened my resolve to bring forward a plan that I had long kept secret.

When you are at the end of the world, in no country, and your way home could be across any couple of oceans, it is easy to dream. Distances are relative and the truth is that Africa, Australia and America are all quite close. But if you have an ocean for each point of the compass and a boat at your fingertips, dreaming wastes time. Better to get under way.

The wicked red line that appeared on my revered *National Geographic Atlas of the World* would have shocked anyone accustomed to measuring distances in kilometres and annotating only in pencil. Incredible; my onward route would bear no resemblance to the one I had taken when coming here. And though *Paratii* would still be held fast in ice for months longer she was already, in spirit, sailing at high speed, in the opposite direction.

Silence and peace. Not necessarily a tranquil peace. Reading at night in front of the heater, listening to my favourite records was no longer my idea of peace. To finish the task of mapping out the crevasses at the summit of the island, and then come skiing home at high speed was what brought me peace. Or to examine the mooring ropes secured to the 'flat stone'. Other things, though, worried me; the safety anchor to the north, which I had not seen because it was hidden beneath the ice, and the ropes fastened around the 'south rock'.

Now the batteries were charged only twice a week, once using the generator and once from the main engine. These were fantastic nickel-cadmium alkaline batteries, especially made by Nife in São Paulo. They had been designed to put up with considerable abuse, but remained always perfectly charged. There were two banks for general use and two banks to power the starter motor, and they were intended to be part of the ship's ballast. Through months of darkness, they ran the amplifiers at full blast for innumerable parties, powered the radios for endless communication sessions and handled all forms of conspicuous power consumption on board without protest.

The problem of condensation and icing on the hatches was perfectly resolved. It hadn't been practical to use double glazing while building the boat, and instead I brought some plastic sheeting to fix on to the window frames with double-sided Scotch tape. A simple, nifty solution. A different solution for the seven windows in the cockpit was needed, since ice was forming along the inside of their metallic frames due to heat exchange. I cut two-inch strips of styrofoam (the same material used to insulate the rest of the boat) and fixed them on the inside. After all this glazing work, the average indoor temperature had risen by almost 4°C, a considerable saving of heating fuel.

One unforgivable oversight happened after my last bath. I forgot to drain the electric heater, so the water froze and the shower cracked from side to side. I had already done the same stupid thing with the spare electric shower. After that I had to make do with a splash-bath in the bows, a lot more fun than those crazy showers. Because the pipes and water tanks were frozen, the biggest problem was collecting and heating the water beforehand, melting snow off the deck or sea-ice over the stove.

The worst job was washing the clothes. Worse even than spending the whole day freezing down in the engine room, changing the oil or greasing exposed mechanical parts. To do a day's washing, I had to spend at least four days melting snow. Longing thoughts of those summer days when I had plied the washer-woman's trade out there on the rocks, shirtless and in dark glasses, using that natural pool of running water now buried under three or four metres of snow.

A solution also was found for the ice that froze on the decking after 'hot' days. I can't remember which genius had made me stow a rubber hammer on board, like truck drivers use. It was a magical way to get rid of the ice without completely demolishing *Paratii* in the process. A couple of hours of demented battering with the rubber hammer, hair flying, cursing the warmth of freezing point, surprising the penguins who always drew closer to watch, and there – a new boat. Afterwards, of course, I had to sweep away the broken ice shards before they froze on to the deck all over again. This job became known as 'visiting Laura's psychoanalyst'.

Years before, one Saturday morning, I'd had a row with my friend Laura Falzoni. She was still angry when she found me later that day in the little mews in front of another friend Beto Haenel's house. We were organising a street party. In the middle of the road was a large lump of concrete which had been there for decades and was expected to be there for ever. Angry, super-elegant and enigmatic as ever, Laura got out of her car without saying a word, seized a ten-pound sledge-hammer and demolished the lump during an impressive fifteen-minute show. Shards of concrete flew everywhere and her hair stood on end as she delivered blow after blow under the startled gaze of the neighbours, until the lump was turned into dust. When she threw down the hammer, wild and panting, Beto, who had not understood what was happening, asked:

'What's going on, Laura?'

'Nothing,' she said, looking at me as she fixed her hair. 'I've just saved some bucks at the analyst's. Bye!' and she left.

'Laura's psychoanalyst' had to get to work more than once a week during May, a month full of snowstorms, heat and icing over. Yet I found a strange kind of peace, full of tools and screws all over the floor, repairs and alterations, wires and ropes all over the place, as well as skis and sledges piled up outside and tracks leading everywhere through the snow. Piles of books to be read; inventions, ideas and lists of what I would need, to carry out my still-secret plan.

At the end of the month, on one of those rare days of

complete calm, I noted in the diary, page seventy-four: 'How I miss you, dear sun, I hadn't even noticed your disappearance.'

A fantastic moon for most of the day – no daylight any more, but I hardly noticed. Only a clear, red-tinged sky for a few hours, then a long night. Sunset and sunrise had united in a single brief effort of light at around midday. We were heading for the middle of the long winter and as the winter solstice approached, the non-scientific weather-forecasting techniques lost all their meaning.

Red sky at night, sailor's delight
Red sky in the morning, sailor's warning.

Colourful mornings and evenings were the same, and when the moon came up, night was brighter than day. I bid my dark glasses adieu until the following summer.

In the 'dark and gloomy polar winter' there is much more light than I had expected. The sea, its frozen surface covered in snow, reflects every drop of light, and the starry sky, even when there is no moon, makes an excellent companion for long walks. Dangerous glaciers that previously I had feared to approach were now harmless ghosts, trapped by the sea, illuminated by moonlight.

The snow, constantly swept away by strong winds, became scarce now and would only lie on the land. So I had to start hauling snow regularly to make fresh water. On skis, with a rope about my waist, pulling the latest model sledge.

At the start of June, the temperature finally fell to around minus 14°C. Fair weather and clear skies returned. And on the first Tuesday of the month such an extraordinary full moon shone over my domain that I thought I would have to bring out a pair of darkened 'moon glasses'. Instead of going to bed, I went for a long walk, crossing over the first of the peaks on 'my' island that could be seen from the boat. From the top the view was spectacular. The Neumayer Channel was all white, even though the sea-ice didn't look hard; the two bays on either side of the Damoy Peninsula and its channels looked completely frozen, though. Down below, the little lamp inside *Paratii*, cast its glow over the white snow. My comfortable, beloved wandering home.

I went out without skis now, taking only an aluminium shovel and, to get back down to Dorian Bay I chose the steepest hillside, sat on the shovel, and, holding on to the handle, using both feet as directional brakes, hurtled down at great speed coming to a snow-covered stop beside the Weddell seal who lived near *Paratii*. She was on the ice, and lifted her head to watch, but remained otherwise indifferent to my antics. It was as clear as a summer's day, but with the negative clarity of darkness reflected in the frozen sea. I yelled aloud but, perhaps because of the snow, there was no echo. During the night a haze developed, so fine as to be almost imperceptible, which formed a halo around the moon, or rather a circular rainbow, all the colours of the spectrum. In a chapter devoted to optical phenomena, the *Antarctic Pilot* discusses lunar peculiarities such as 'parselenae, lunar haloes, coronas and aureolas'. But I never imagined such things would be so ravishing.

'Good grief, there's no way I'm sleeping!' I made a rapid attack on the kitchen, and went out with my photographic equipment for a few hours of photographic experiment. I moved the tripod several times until I had finished all the rolls of film. Standing beside the boat, heaving up the camera bag, and for no good reason, I took out the only camera that still had some film in it, a diver's Nikonos. Taking three steps back for a last shot, the ice suddenly gave way and down I went, camera and all. There wasn't even time to use the metal hooks sewn into my wristband, designed for accidents like this. I shot out of the water quicker than a penguin and rushed on board with boots full of water and clothes drenched. With all that extra weight I was unable to leap on to the deck as normal, and had to slither on board like a seal. Within thirty seconds I was naked by the heater, my wet clothes hanging by the door, a towel on my shoulders and thick, dry socks on my feet, a bottle of Bordeaux already opened, laughing my head off.

What luck, or rather, what a warning to have fallen in while carrying the diver's camera. Nothing like a compulsory bath to put you to sleep like an angel. I woke up late the following day. I could hear *Vagabundo*, the little dinghy, deflated, flapping in the wind where it lay up on deck. I thought it was getting impatient for the day – whenever that might be – we would put to sea.

My mind was on other things. It was 12 June, the Brazilian St Valentine's day.

The snow fell horizontally, icy, dark. I spent the day organising my collection of screws. I switched on the recorder to tape the weather synopsis transmitted on the ship-radio frequency by Palmer Station, I pressed the wrong button and tuned in to a station from southern Brazil. In the middle of the World Cup, airwaves saturated with football, here was a completely zany programme in which the only rule was that no one could mention that dreary, rule-bound game called football. Instead it was a sort of free association by a sophisticated group of broadcasters from Rio Grande do Sul in southern Brazil. I recorded a scrap of it and later listened to it hundreds of times.

*   *   *

Vibrating in the wind, during a bad-tempered gust, the hull freed itself from the ice slipping in its icy mould, and heeled over further and further. Several times the instruments showed she was tilting over as much as twenty-five degrees. Odd to be leaning over like this without going anywhere, just slithering around in a big ice-bucket. I turned off the radio, it was too noisy. The rudder was worrying me too, because of the strains on it. I should have taken it off, but it was too late. Deafening, icy wind, complete darkness. Below decks the real damage was confined to my little garden of alfalfa sprouts, radish and *moyashi*, all of which almost flew up the wall. The blizzard raged for ten hours, without doing any lasting damage. Then the temperature dropped and everything returned to normal.

On the eve of the mid-winter solstice, 20 June, the warm weather was back. This time it didn't come alone. Strong winds and, unfortunately, high tides. The whole bay began to move and huge cracks appeared in its surface. *Paratii* broke away from her bed in the ice and began to beat against the ice sheet, sometimes threatening to ride on top of it. Eventually the ice broke. Huge blows. This time it meant trouble. Immensely thick pieces of ice had broken free and began to entangle themselves in the mooring ropes, beating violently against them, interlinked like some huge jigsaw puzzle, with slack between the pieces.

We were afloat again, in this confusing mixture that wasn't exactly sea and, to add to the confusion, the north-westerly wind, which had blown pieces of ice into the bay, suddenly swung round to the south-west, taking with it pieces of the jigsaw puzzle that had been piling up against the rocks or piling up in the Neumayer Channel. Every gust of wind seemed stronger now that the boat was loose. *Paratii* would rear against the ice sheet or an iceberg, and then slither back and hit another – or rather the rudder would hit it. I disconnected the rudder cables in order to reduce the damage, but I just didn't know what to do about the rudder blade. Should I try and unship it in the middle of that chaos, or lash it? I didn't have the slightest idea. For the second time I regretted not having dismantled it before the bad weather. Patience.

Two days of chaos, blows, with two gigantic icebergs stuck at the bows and the stern from which I couldn't get free. Tons of ice dragged the boat, the mooring ropes screaming ceaselessly. The rudder was making such a racket I decided – a brilliant idea – to lash it to the tiller bar. It was quiet for a few seconds and then – crack – the bar snapped like a biscuit; a two-inch welded pipe with a half-inch inner seam. Nothing too serious; I had two spare bars that crazy Eduardo had insisted on making up. But I did not enjoy seeing part of my rudder turn into biscuit crumbs. Those two days struggling with the mooring ropes and the ice in the deafening roar of the wind gave me plenty to think about.

The greatest challenge to ships spending the winter in the ice had never been simply the pressure generated by the ice, or its expansion during the cold period. Shackleton's *Endurance* survived 281 days adrift and held fast in the frozen Weddell Sea until it was abandoned. Nansen's revolutionary ship *Fram*, designed for winter sojourns by the brilliant Colin Archer, had spent a total of seven years drifting in the Arctic ice before she travelled with Amundsen to the South Pole. There were two expeditions: Nansen's famous voyage from 1893 to 1896; and another from 1898 to 1902 under Otto Sverdrup's command.

During the 'heroic' period of Antarctic exploration the leading polar ships of the day were sealers or Norwegian whaling ships: this was true of Gerlache's *Belgica*, previously named the *Patria*; and of Shackleton's *Endurance*; likewise the German ship *Gauss*, also designed by Colin Archer; and both the French ships belonging to Dr Charcot, *Le Français* and the *Pourquoi Pas?*. The experience of all these ships in their winter sojourns confirmed that the real danger does not come from the slow increase in pressure from the ice, but from the movement of the ice sheet when plates of it become broken or loose. So the thaw when winter ends is much more dangerous than the big freeze. A sharply inclined, wedge-like hull obviously helps during prolonged periods of high pressure, because the boat is simply pushed upwards and out of the ice. This shape also helps in the case of sudden blows to the side of the boat by either forcing the boat to rise up or the ice to slide down. This is a risky moment for any boat, and one which I had only expected to encounter at the start of next summer.

I disliked this brutal, unseasonable thaw. It lasted two days, and seemed longer than the six months since I had left Jurumirim. And the long-awaited party to celebrate the winter solstice had to be cancelled for lack of ice – and humour. But on the third day, when the winds dropped and Dorian Bay was again covered with a fine coating of new snow, there was a truck-load of reasons for a party.

Half of my Antarctic dream had been accomplished with the arrival of the solstice. Just as if it had passed the lowest point in a valley, the sun's journey across the sky would take it a little higher each day, until one day it would finally reappear above my horizon. But the other half of my dream was still far away.

Paratii had shown her strength during those interminable forty-eight hours. Barely 100 metres away sheets of ice weighing thousands of tonnes had been piled like cardboard in one corner of the bay. There were scratches on the hull where the paint had been scraped away, but that was all. A boat built out of any other material but aluminium would not have survived so well. There was no visible damage apart from these scratches and some zinc anodes wrenched off. Though the rudder had been banging away like a jazz drummer in Joe Morello's version of 'Take Five' (and had even broken its drumsticks), it was intact.

I'd passed most of this interminable concert in a cold sweat, praying that time would spin forward, allow me to escape the torture of waiting, the agony of not knowing how long I had to wait, the tension of simply having to wait. But there are no half-measures. Maybe this is the real pleasure of riding out the storm: you only reach the good weather by passing through every second that precedes it. There are no shortcuts. I would only see the sun again having endured the whole winter, without missing a day. I could only get home to Paraty by crossing every degree of latitude, every single mile of my route.

The days were transformed into places, the hours and minutes became tiny spots or fractions of these places. Time, which I had been used to measuring on the calendar, could not be counted any more. It was like a machine hurtling along with no brakes, speeding through every place without stopping. A red vehicle in which I was the only passenger.

9

ON THE FAR SIDE OF THE ICE

Seventeen vipers and two cobras devouring my beloved Japanese screwdriver! What a disaster! But there was still time to go on a hunting expedition to the 'Butantan Institute' – the snake farm. Most of the things that had mysteriously disappeared on board had fallen into the reptile pit at the 'Institute'– *Paratii*'s central cockpit, which held the rudder wheel and where all the ropes and cables for manoeuvring the boat converged – a layout especially designed for single-handed sailing. With the exception of the mainsail sheets, which I controlled from the mast, all other ropes were controlled from the protection and safety of the cockpit. For each manoeuvre, there was a rope, nineteen in all, and, on the days of great sailing activity, they would become more or less poisonous, getting entwined and sometimes, grabbing my boots.

During the winter, with the boat laid up, the 'Institute' was transformed into a kind of dump where I threw my skis on returning home. Buckets, spades, pickaxes and less delicate implements were stored there too. As it was always covered in snow, any small object that slipped in would disappear among the ice and the frozen 'snakes' lying on the bottom. I could have unrigged *Paratii*, bringing down all her sails and folding them and then removing all the ropes, organised the lot and stored everything inside the boat. But where? Certainly not in the main cabin where I lived and which was wonderfully warm and more or less tidy. The volume of sails and rope would be huge and the amount of work even greater. Although the most excessively traditional sailors in Brazil had guaranteed that the cold would destroy any fabric left outside the boat, such as sails or rope, I knew that handling them in the intense cold on my own, folding and unfolding them, would be a great deal worse. So I left everything exactly as it had been on the day I arrived, simply covering the sails with UV light protectors. The sails remained in their furling reefs, everything ready to leave, and I was happy about that.

But the 'snake farm' could not be spared, and must succumb to an investigation of its heap. The previous evening I had left the Japanese screwdriver on the side, after adjusting the bindings on my skis, and it must have been blown inside by the snow. Removing the snow, ice and frozen 'snakes', opening the way with a shovel and pickaxe, I made several archaeological finds of great interest: a half-opened packet of biscuits I had been feeding to the albatrosses on the Drake Passage; a lens cap that had been missing for months; a fork; a little roll of pliable stainless-steel wire I'd been hunting desperately for; and a single Neoprene glove – but no screwdriver.

An intense light filled the sky, similar to a sunset. Soon the sun would be back again. I dug deeper into my excavations, hunting the screwdriver, and noticed an unusual agitation among the gentoos. During the stormy days of July they had retreated to Casabianca Island, but now they were slowly coming back towards *Paratii*. First came a single penguin up to the boat and paused for a few seconds to watch me hitting those frozen ropes. Then three more appeared from the opposite direction down by the bay, where they rarely went. They seemed busily engaged on some mysterious mission.

I wouldn't say I understood them perfectly, but I was being treated, at least, with a certain respect already. It had taken me some time to learn how to cross their domain without provoking a racket in the neighbourhood. At first, even when I walked very slowly, step by step behind the door, like a spy, they would get me, they would scream and come running at me. Then I realised that rhythm and style of movement were more important to them in identifying strangers than the speed of movement. I discovered I could pass them running like a madman, as long as I imitated their jerky little steps, looking like Chaplin at high speed. Luckily there were no witnesses. Had there been, I might have had difficulty convincing them of my sanity. No. I hadn't turned into a penguin, much less was I suffering from boredom or struggling with 'terrible Antarctic solitude'.

In fact, I was incredibly well, a bit surprised and in a bit of a hurry, much like the gentoos living beside me. In seven months, I couldn't remember two days the same. Nothing going on around me could be compared to anything I had seen before. The snow, always different, the sea-ice now completely irregular, with strange, rounded forms trapped in it. Transformations were ceaseless; the volume of light, the colour of days, even the landscape. Gigantic icebergs made their way down the Neumayer Channel, making a fantastic racket as they cut their way through the sea-ice, driven not by the wind but by strong currents in the channel. One of these monsters, which must have been over fifty metres high at its peak, had gone aground in front of me, its strange colours transforming the landscape around me. Although I am not at all keen on dancing, I surprised myself many times making artistic efforts to the sound of a crazy record of *forró* music from the north-east of Brazil. And of course, with a floor-cloth under my boots, I could dry out the snow which I'd carried on board at the same time.

Sometimes I worked like a slave just to carry on living, not to let the mess and the jobs pile up like the snow on deck. But, when everything was finished, I would amuse myself like a prince. Nothing worked properly by chance – the engine, heater, power, lights, the lagging, water supply, galley and all the rest needed constant attention. The great pleasure was that there were no superfluous tasks. Even grumbling at the end of the day because I hadn't yet found the screwdriver, I knew that next day I would find it, and anyway, I would have have domesticated and organised those 'snakes'.

In fact, next morning I found my screwdriver, and made at lunch a noisy celebration. Fresh salad with vegetables from the experimental garden, pizza – with pastry from the continental bakery, which was now operating twice a week – and homemade cheese, all served on a check tablecloth with a good wine. After all, it was a pleasant Saturday and the ice was quiet. From any aspect, my red residence was an agreeable place.

There were, of course, some privations. I badly missed the muddle of home, my crazy friends, the trees I had planted in the most unlikely places, those journeys I was always taking – but no way was I suffering. Other madmen, perhaps not so friendly, were far away, there would be no lack of travels before arriving home, and trees, OK, they were just a question of latitude and patience.

I raced through this period at great speed, in the direction already fixed and plotted, without being able to stop or turn back. I remembered the letter from my friend Hélio Setti which I had read many times and had been so important during my journey. Miserably it had vanished months before, probably tucked into some book or corner so as not to lose it.

The letter dealt with the question of time. Time hadn't stopped as I had thought it might, while *Paratii* had been in the ice. In fact I became neither master nor slave of time, as Hélio had predicted. But I discovered that I could 'direct' my time, to force all these separate moments to flow in a particular direction. To transform the months and the seconds that were distant, into a real destination. The few occasions when I let time take charge of itself, when I had no clear idea of what I should do apart from getting away, turned out to be slow days of flat calm, of terrible weather, of bad moods. No and no again. A million times I would rather face the worst storm than these tepid periods of drift and calm, going nowhere.

Strangely, these were the only days I felt lonely: when I set aside my plans and drifted, allowing things to happen without understanding how and where they would end up.

Now things were different. Even if it was in a cemetery, I knew where I would end up if I was distracted, made errors, or let the boat drift. I knew the sun would be back, and that one day the ice would break up and I would be able to continue my journey.

Like the winter, living cut off by ice was not a permanent condition. I hadn't been abandoned here in Dorian Bay. And I wasn't escaping from anything, or needing to prove skills or ability. Nor was I turning my back on consumer society. Or trying to know my inner self or test humanity's further limits – none of that rubbish. It was just that this was what I most desired in the world. To spend a whole year on my own. Just once. And why exactly? I hadn't the faintest idea. All I knew was that though I was passing a period in solitary, I felt no solitude. I felt closer than ever to dear friends, the distance between us was just physical. An emotional distance that I knew how to cross. True solitude, an interior distance, between people sometimes close to each other, abandonment, lack of objective, of will-power, of support: I knew nothing of this. I felt sure that even creditors, accountants and vindictive enemies, if they existed, would hope for *Paratii*'s speedy return. Every screw, every piece, every detail of my world, spoke of the care and concern of someone: the detailed woodwork that Arnaldo had painstakingly created; the thousands of small stainless-steel parts and components invented and manufactured by Celsão; Chris's rare book, Japanese amulets by Issao Kohara, the engine perfectly installed by the Perkins team after so much effort – hundreds of stories, cases and funny accidents, showing that no boat is built by one man alone and that even a crew of one is not alone.

Not to be able to share special moments, might have been a problem, but at sea, there are certain situations not to be shared. Some so beautiful and unique that they should continue within the person who experienced them and only then be transmitted: entire. Other difficulties, fear and panic, are not helped by more people. Alone, for moments only, I saw things and experienced situations whose particular beauty I will keep with me all my life. But I also went through bad moments that I would not wish on any friend. And it was alone – for these brief moments that lasted a winter – that I learned how to make time move faster so that people and places, those we long for and miss so much, could be reached much sooner.

It is difficult to explain where ideas come from. Sometimes as a reaction to a simple word: 'impossible'.

I heard once a ship's captain, also a single-handed yachtsman who knew Antarctica well, telling of his adventures and achievements: 'It's impossible to sail on your own down there, completely impossible,' he said. Extraordinary what a great capacity human beings have for building obstacles. The most religious of animals is the least credulous, and is also the one with the greatest facility for inventing excuses for not changing, for opposing things, and for inventing insurmountable obstacles that in reality have no more significance than a line drawn with chalk on the ground. A hundred years ago, before Joshua Slocum's extraordinary voyage of circumnavigation, perhaps, but today, what is impossible? Interesting, and relative this word.

Until a short time ago, anyone who could have envisaged the most out-of-date microwave oven, or who had talked about the possibilities of the most primitive of today's computers, would have been excommunicated and condemned as a witch, or condemned to slavery, in the galleys. The worst sin we may commit in the future will be of omission, for the means already exist to do many beautiful and impossible things.

The previous experience of yachtsmen in Antarctica has been fascinating. Up till now only three sailing boats had overwintered in Antarctica. The last had been *Dick Smith Explorer*, a 65-foot-long steel-built Australian yacht belonging to Dr David Lewis. The vessel spent the winter in the Rauer Islands in the Australian sector on the other side of Antarctica, with six people aboard (four men and two women). It was a controversial experience, filled with arguments, accusations and misunderstandings. Technically successful, the enterprise could inspire no one. The same Dr Lewis had been the first single-handed sailor to go down to Antarctica, in 1972–3, aboard his tiny 33-foot yacht *Icebird*. The boat was laid up through the winter at Palmer Station, and the following year he came back by ship to take the yacht onward to Cape Town. A disastrous journey. Out of it he produced a book full of absurd bits of advice and lessons for all polar sailors, which I consider to be the Bible of all one should NEVER do in Antarctic waters or how never to behave while at bases on the continent.

The second winter sojourn took place in 1981–2, some forty miles south of *Paratii*, at Petermann Island. Afterwards the boat passed through Rio de Janeiro, and its four male crew members left behind an interesting and enjoyable account of their experiences.

But the beautiful voyage, almost magical, which

enchanted me was the first, that of Sally and Jérôme Poncet, on board *Damien II*, a sailing boat made in the same shipyard which built *Rapa Nui*, and which gave birth to a series of boats, a philosophy of life and a story. I knew them in Rio and Jérôme gave me an old anemometer that I still have. Afterwards, I met them again with Oleg and Sophie, another couple with great Antarctic experience, whose boat *Kotic* is a sister ship of *Damien II*. Jérôme, a true Breton, silent and active, and Sally, a beautiful and strong Australian, completed their journey giving birth to a son, Dion, born on board, in complete isolation. They had two more children and have never stopped returning to the icy continent – always in the rusty, now legendary *Damien II*. It was they, without any heroics, who discovered all the safe anchorages across Antarctica that small boats make use of today.

More than invaluable counsel; from them I caught the virus that eventually brought me to Dorian Bay.

Maybe because of this, I spent the days humming obscenities, making all kinds of art, thinking non-stop, challenging the heaps of nautical maps and calculations covering the chart table every night. And every day, closer and more certain, the departure date.

On 20 July, Friday, at 13.15, local time, the sun returned after a 58-day absence. 'Old Jamaica' rides again! A few seconds, but unforgettable. Real sunlight illuminated *Paratii*, coming in the windows, casting long shadows of penguins across the snow. A party. Seven minutes of sun. A big unforgettable party for the return of the sun. Just knowing it was there, even without seeing it, would have been the same.

I tested out the new rudder bar, whose repair had taken two weeks' work, and a pair of Canadian skis that were used for both cross-country and downhill. I went to the 'supermarket' at the forward hold for the 'shopping trip' for my thirty-first week or eighth month, where I found many interesting goodies. On the Saturday, finally, I plunged down into *Paratii*'s bilges to check the fuel. Each load of twenty litres of diesel for the heater allowed, on average, eleven days of comfort; an approximate consumption of sixty litres a month. There was still enough fuel for another ten months of heating, without rationing. In the two main tanks, there was enough of the two-to-one mixture of diesel/white kerosene to motor for 1,200 miles. Not bad. Self-sufficiency in fuel is vital for life in Antarctica, and the source of relative peace of mind for anyone who has plans to move on. Snowing or not, hot or cold, good weather in these parts usually means no wind, so moving around almost always means using the motor.

Down in the 'catacombs' under the floor I discovered a second likely repository for all those objects that had mysteriously disappeared or been forgotten. Strange things I couldn't remember any more, such as an orange-coloured chain-saw, especially designed to cut ice or even concrete. It had a long blade and an extraordinarily wide chain I hoped I would never have to use. Down there under the decking was a small outboard motor. I don't know why, but I decided to store it in the galley and, curiosity aroused, I opened the engine cover to see if the tools and spare propeller were all there to find a little rubber grommet used for storing the spare split-pins which held the propeller on to the shaft. There was one pin and two empty holes. Even though I was covered in oil and grease from the inspection of the fuel tanks and had no idea why I was doing this, I went to the workshop to find a piece of stainless-steel bar. Inside half an hour I made three new pins complete with chamfered points. Opa! Without meaning to, I even made an extra one. I was going to throw it away because there was no extra space for it in the rubber grommet, but instead put it inside the little bag containing the spare spark plug and tools. I closed the lid and put everything away. It would be months until I used that outboard again and I had no way of foreseeing that the last and seemingly unnecessary split-pin would one day save my neck.

Filthy, exhausted but the happy owner of eighty litres of running water, I treated myself to a full bath, wash and brush-up on the bow, and then jumped into the most comfortable bed I could ever remember.

The following morning, a freezing Sunday in August, a heroic determination was needed to get me out of my sleeping bag. I don't know why, always on Sundays, the weather decides to bare its teeth, but today there must be a problem. There was a torrid sun and a celestial calm. Brushing my teeth, I received a shock: strange character in the mirror, clean, shaven and shorn . . .

My faithful neighbour, Barbara, the Weddell seal, turned out to be in pup. And perhaps had marriage problems, because all the other seals were in Port Lockroy, looking after their breathing-holes in the ice and, no doubt, sunning themselves on such a pleasant day.

While I was collecting samples, I was surprised by a new visitor. An enormous elephant seal, still young, very timid and easily frightened, unlike Barbara, who enjoyed showing off and posing for photos. Separated from a family of elephant seals over to the south of Anvers Island, where there was a large colony, in ten seconds he was called Theobald. Discreet and completely silent, he became the third mammal resident in Dorian Bay.

The penguin population grew from one hour to the next. Many hundreds of them now, wandering about everywhere, sometimes following my ski-tracks, sometimes nibbling at the boat's rudder. They massed around certain spots, to which they would always return.

How sad this place would be without the presence of the animals. Any life-form in Antarctica must be admired, for survival in such an inhospitable place is not easy.

Sometimes I would think about the incredible efficiency and balance between the species that live together here; and what teeth for example, Barbara must have to enable her to keep permanently open a breathing-hole in a half-metre-thick ice sheet. Older animals simply die when their teeth are no longer strong enough to keep doing this job.

What incredible agility and elegance a seal had under the ice, catching enough food to sustain a bulk of 300–400 kilos. Incredible, too, was the amount of effort the same animal needed to haul itself over the stones on the seashore. The gentoos' competitive warblings, interrupted every now and then by the guttural comments of the Adélie penguins in transit through the bay. Few birds had remained here over the winter, but many would soon return, already their footprints and ski-trails could be seen everywhere. Other, heavier marks appeared in the snow; some made by mammals like Theobald, who left a trail like a bulldozer as he lumbered from place to place – all this brought a crescendo of animation to life in Dorian Bay, which matched the return of the sun.

As the sun's declination increased with the arrival of spring, the short days and winter winds seemed far behind me.

Storms raged through the month of August, occasionally interrupted by spectacularly beautiful days. But as *Paratii* was still fast in the ice, I wasn't worried by them. I became a sun-worshipper and in homage to this great star, took on all the sordid and unpleasant tasks on board. The worst of these was to clean up *Paratii*'s 'catacombs' – removing the ice that had built up in the hold and testing all the boat's valves. The ice down there – composed of condensation and accumulated rubbish – was sticky and disgusting. I had to have a little taste to see if it was salty and so check there was no leakage. It was revolting but there was no leakage, thank God. A serious detail. I discovered that one of the hoses had cracked from contracting in the cold, so I quickly replaced it with the help of my favourite blow torch. Low temperatures, ranging from $-8°C$ to $-20°C$, ensured a dry, comfortable climate. Returning home after long skiing expeditions, I was almost always wearing only a T-shirt, with coat and jumper tied around the waist.

In spite of so many abrupt changes in the weather or light, the comings and goings of birds and seals, the shifting moods of the ice, life pursued its course in a natural and harmonious rhythm.

I was infected by the activity in the neighbourhood. Working on *Paratii* was no longer maintaining her safety while the ice persisted, but getting her ready to sail again. To sail far away.

When summer returned, I hoped to spend six weeks visiting anchorages and places I hadn't yet seen using many drawings and plans given to me by Jérôme and Sally, travelling to Lagoon Island in Marguerite Bay. Only then would I confirm plans for the return.

But during the now-vanishing winter I had already decided not to return to Brazil. If the ice broke before Christmas, I could have been back home by the following January. But after months that had gone by so quickly, next January seemed horribly, unfairly close. Having begun this voyage almost overwhelmed with the prospect of the long months that stretched before, now I was restless, anxious at the short space of time that remained before my winter sojourn was over. The prospect of the thaw perhaps two months away was also making me nervous. The shapes of both Dorian Bay and the Neumayer Channel were very different now; the ice no longer formed a smooth sheet, but had an irregular surface in which large blocks were held. Two jutting monsters had fused themselves with my mooring lines and would doubtless break apart in spectacular fashion when the thaw came.

One year is a curious measure of time. So many years

are lost by people who live cautiously, thinking about the future, seeking security and, without being aware of it, dying by inches without doing anything significant. Here, in one brief year, so many experiences and events had piled up that it would be impossible to describe and record them all simply by following the chronological unfolding of the calender. I started sketching out the calendar for the next three months, using block capitals on squared paper which I planned to fix to the bulkhead by the chart table, but ended up adding a larger sheet of paper and extending the calendar to cover the next twelve months.

I resolved not to hurry home, and to gain a year in my voyage.

To return as I had secretly dreamed before leaving Jurumirim, a dream now coming closer and closer. Leaving the Antarctic ice, and before returning to Brazil, I would follow the path of the migratory terns as far as the Arctic ice-cap, the long way home. To the other end of the earth, and, who knows, the far side of the ice.

10

THE FRAGMENTED BAY

' Oh my God! There she is.' I put the binoculars inside my rucksack, slipped the straps of my ski-sticks around my wrists and sped off in the direction of a shovel I'd left five months ago, on top of the mountain. It was marking one of the treacherous crevasses I had discovered on the overland route to Port Lockroy: an enormous and deep fissure already, at that time of the year, covered by snow bridges, which, at the least slip, would swallow up a passer-by. For ever.

The shovel had barely been covered by the snows, and the handle was still visible. I'd used it to dig an underground shelter, a kind of igloo carved in the snow that I would sometimes visit, always armed to the teeth with skis, sticks and a long probe to explore the snow in front, in search of crevasses. I loved the place. What an extraordinary view! On a sunny day like this, the landscape became altered by the refraction of light from the white surface creating a fascinating arc of distorted shapes. I'd spend hours admiring the mountains and peaks, while, at the bottom of the slope, were the ruins of the old base and, on the other side, my own ski-tracks leading back to that minuscule and distant red object fast in the frozen ice. If it was windy, I would get inside the igloo illuminated by a strange blueish glow piercing the snow. Inside, a chamber of absolute silence.

But by now the old igloo was almost covered and I had no time to start digging it out again. I had to get back to the boat quickly because in an hour, at 14:30 local time, 16:30 GMT, I had planned a radio communication with Alvaro, on a special frequency so that I could tell Hermann my new plan.

A long time before we had agreed on a very special plan. Hermann was, perhaps even more than myself, completely in love with the blue schooner, *Rapa Nui*, and he also dreamed of a journey to Antarctica. While *Paratii* was being built, he completely dismantled and rebuilt the blue boat so that we could learn the characteristics of her construction. He knew the boat better than anyone and it was agreed he would prepare her and, in December, lead a four-man crew down to Antarctica before I left. A beautiful idea.

Rapa Nui and *Paratii* together again, side by side in the ice, just as they were at the Hanseática dockyard in Guarujá or at Jurumirim, surrounded by trees. But it was also to be a strategic encounter. *Rapa Nui* was to bring the navigational documents, new almanacs, pilot charts and maps I would be needing if I wished to sail non-stop northwards. She would also bring a fresh stock of film and batteries for the equipment and take home unneeded material left over from the winter sojourn. There was, however, a complication: Hermann had no experience of deep-water navigation or long-distance sailing, in spite of all the extensive journeys we had made together along the Brazilian coast in a number of decrepit vessels. It would be a tricky journey with other people on board, demanding attention. Both of us were worried about it. On the other hand, there was no one in the world I would rather have entrusted *Rapa Nui* to. Almost nobody in Brazil had any experience at all of cold-water sailing. But, in the end what counts at sea even more than experience, is having initiative, respect and the ability to learn. I trusted my friend, partner and fellow oarsman from university days. Whole flotillas of wise and experienced sailors sitting on their club terraces or grand-looking toy boats would never know how to sail in high latitudes or beyond well-charted seas. This, at least, Hermann knew.

This communication gave birth to a list of orders that grew week by week, together with a delicious sense of expectancy that drew the boats closer. If they could leave at the beginning of December, they might arrive by Christmas that year. Surrounded by snow and ice, the pilothouse on *Paratii* and its radio desk became a hive of planning activity. The truth was, a change of plans for my return had to some extent been foreseen. Self-sufficiency was the crucial logistical detail that allowed *Paratii* to opt for a completely different route. Autonomy; something I would never give up for anything in the world. An audit of supplies carried out in September had revealed that without any undue rationing I would have been able to survive another winter, in terms of fuel, spare parts and maintenance equipment. The dental kit, supplied by Fêca, my dentist friend, hadn't even been touched, even though I could have carried out all kinds of emergency repairs and operations if needed. All had been studied and rehearsed: fillings, anaesthetics and several manoeuvres grisly enough just to imagine, though I would not be caught unprepared. What the dentist probably never imagined was that I would become wholly reliant on his mirrors and orthodontic instruments to check electrical connections on the radios, or to assess the state of the inaccessible screws in the engine room.

In the cabinet, there was another work of art: a pharmacy and first-aid clinic, both portable and carefully put together by another friend, Edison Mantovani. We had already travelled together and raced in regattas. The only problem was the look of surprise that I got from the other patients in his waiting-room when I went to consult my doctor. Edison is a gynaecologist.

The seal on the medicine cabinet had only been broken because Edison had included in it an absolutely irresistible orthopaedic kit filled with all kinds of fantastic material for putting plaster on broken limbs, and other emergency care. With my tool box, the orthopaedics kit and a little patience I could easily have built a whole new boat if *Paratii* had been crushed by the ice.

The first patient for Edison's pharmacy was Barbara the seal, who had cut one of her flippers, probably while trying to cross over rocks and ice against the tide.

After I had finished talking to Hermann, I went out to put a thick layer of cream on Barbara and the sheath bill which was pecking at her wound, went away.

For the purposes of planning, the greatest guarantee of self-sufficiency aboard *Paratii* was the supply of food. Just planning the provisions was a task every bit as complex as building the boat itself and it had begun even before the boat existed. Four years of work. Tests, tastings, endless experiments, all to ensure the stomach's good working order. Flora, a well-known nutrition specialist, had directed the job at Nutrimental, her old company. Under the supervision of Takako, a Japanese woman tougher than a general but with a sweet disposition, a friendly and hard-working group of nutritionists and food technicians produced a complete programme of meals for three and a half years of travel. There would be no need of extra supplies, replacements or any refrigeration, and everything had to last for five years. Breakfast with fruits and fresh cheese, fresh salad, a beef strogonoff, chicken pie or a fresh pitta-bread sandwich – to last the next five years, with no tins or freezing, without stepping foot into a supermarket – a real challenge. Almost 90,000 packages, labelled separately with their instructions, nearly

1,000 different items, seven programmes and diets, pans and cutlery, propagators for grains or salads, besides emergency survival provisions, in case I had to abandon the boat. Two cookery and instruction books, each 190 pages long. A show kitchen, in original circumstances, which few good restaurants could equal.

So why three and a half years of self-sufficiency? Simply because in Antarctica it is better to be prepared for the worst. The worst thing imaginable would be not having the option – or the ability if circumstances demanded – of staying another year; or of going off in another direction for another two years.

These preparations were by no means excessive in the light of an involuntary over-wintering. You could say it was an act of faith of the kind that sometimes makes different people get together to go further. As the boat's steward and head cook, I knew I could go far and live well.

Gradually I progressed to lighter and lighter meals, almost cutting out fatty foods altogether, as Flora had expected. This was exactly the opposite of what happens on most polar boats and Antarctic bases, where fatty foods are the rule and almost everyone gets stomach problems, not to mention the phenomenon of overweight researchers. The other advantage was that the washing-up was less of a task – a chore you cannot escape even at the ends of the earth.

Despite all this, when the penultimate Saturday in September came, I opened up the container for week number thirty-five in the hopes of finding more mousses, ice-creams or chocolates than the expected number. Alas, that was wishful thinking.

Since accidentally recording the chat-show on the Brazilian Gaúcha Radio a couple of months before, I had got into the habit of noting down, whenever I was at home, at least one of the coded weather bulletins that

Palmer Station transmitted to the nearby UK base, Faraday. It was a sequence of fifteen to seventeen numbers describing the weather during the six previous hours:

FOUR NINE EIGHT NINE FIVE (PRESSURE 989.5 HP)
FIVE THREE ZERO TWO NINE (INCREASE OF 2.9 HP FOR THE NEXT THREE HOURS)
THREE THREE THREE
ONE ONE ONE FOUR FOUR (MAXIMUM TEM-PERATURE −14.4°C)
TWO ONE ONE SEVEN TWO (MINIMUM TEM-PERATURE −17.2°C) . . .
AND OFF.

Always the same voice. Someone called Ajo, very objective with his information and clear in his pronunciation. Right after the 'and off', he'd have a little chat, telling the day's or the winter's news. Life on these bases is terribly lonely and monotonous, there are restrictions on movement which mean many British researchers, for example, spend two years working shut up in a shed on an island no bigger than a football stadium, without ever travelling more than eight kilometres from the spot, or visiting other Antarctic places. Completely different to the comfort and freedom on board a boat which, once the ice thaws, can go anywhere.

I never wanted to break in, so never made my presence known, but these chats sometimes went on for a long time. And they never knew there was a Brazilian boat spending the winter on the peninsula, and far less, that he was listening in on the 'numbers broadcast'.

On 25 September I got into serious trouble. It was my thirty-fifth birthday and also the day for my weekly radio contact with São Paulo. There was a big party going on in the office, where Cabeluda had organised a celebration.

My friends were gathered around the radio equipment, making a bigger racket than the gentoo penguins as they blew out the candles on my cake, laughing, eating and drinking. There was no escape and though I hoped the celebration would be brief, I joined in, 3,000 miles away. Zezé and my sister made me open letters and little presents that had lain hidden in *Paratii* for nearly a year. I turned the radio off with some relief, a bit overwhelmed. It is not easy to feel so close to people, the most important to you in the world, and yet be so solidly apart.

It was warm again, almost 0°C, and I was sitting in the revolving chair in front of the radio with the door open and my feet outside. A champagne bottle, already half-empty, lay chilling in the snow. It was an extraordinary day and I was thinking how this dark grey box studded with buttons could link me, by way of an antenna, to feelings and people so far away. And through the circuits of this box I was able to develop plans, to hear news and transmissions from all over the world, even to solve the problem of how to blow out the candles on a birthday cake 3,000 miles away.

Lost in thought and with the radio turned off, I almost forgot the Palmer Station weather bulletin. When I turned the radio on and changed wave-band, the numbers were almost ending:

'EIGHT FOUR THREE FIVE SEVEN AND OFF.'

Never mind. I'd get the information another day. There was a short silence in the radio. Suddenly I heard a crackle and . . .

'AMYR . . . AMYR, ARE YOU THERE?'

'Jesus Christ! They're calling me!' I cried in panic. How? How did they find me out? How? The microphone! Where is the microphone?

I flew to the microphone and, almost voiceless, replied. The operator at Palmer, Ajo, had received a message for the Brazilian crew aboard *Paratii*. It came from an old friend on Ilha Grande, PY 1 ZAK, known as 'Peter da Macaca' because he had lived on this island for many years with a female monkey, and the message to Palmer had been transmitted through a complex network of radio hams.

'I can hear you. OK, Amyr, I have a message for you . . . hold on . . . one second please,' said the voice. Five seconds went by, and suddenly a chorus of voices screaming at full volume: 'Happy birthday to you, happy birthday to you . . .'

The guys at Palmer Station singing happy birthday to me; people I knew and anonymous comrades together in the same winter. The end of the world. My heart almost stopped. And so a second cork popped in Dorian Bay and, for the first time, I didn't need to imitate a penguin to look like one. Next day I found a drunken scribble in my diary: 'Don't know how I got home last night.'

*   *   *

At the beginning of spring, the days following the equinox were also to coincide with a lunar quadrature. I was expecting big spring tides and perhaps the break-up of ice around the rocks. But the ice was more than 1.5 metres thick and, during an ebb tide so low that *Paratii* almost touched the bottom, a curious thing happened. The frozen ice sheet of the bay was supported on top of the surrounding rocks and in several places the ice was 'hollow' underneath. That's to say, it was suspended over the sea, producing incredible sounds. The pressure of the ice sheet against the rocks produced a shrill, penetrating sound such as I had never heard before, while under the ice the tiniest movements of water in subterranean galleries would echo with a frightening, amplified sound as though they came from a great imprisoned wave. The tide was so low that the ice around *Paratii* took on the shape of a deep dish. What an opportunity to see the situation of the bow anchor. I went off, without my skis, in Theobald the elephant seal's direction and I found the gap where he had been getting in and out of the water. There was no water left underneath the ice, so I could crawl inside. The only problem was that, if the ice gave in, I'd be flattened like a slug. 'If Theobald managed, why shouldn't I?' I thought, and got in quickly, a little frightened.

It was a crazy sensation. Underneath the frozen sea I went crawling over the rocks, puddles of water, mussels and mud, in quest of the anchor, passing through a natural gallery no more than ninety centimetres high. A blueish light filtered through a roof made of thousands of tons of ice above my back. Silences separated by the deafening sound of breathing and suction when water and ice met. Terrible idea! I was imagining that, if something were to happen, months later someone would find the remains of a human pâté of Brazilian origin, packed in Gore-Tex clothing, beside a beautiful red sailing boat, securely anchored.

And she was secure. I found the anchor in a place where the gap was really low and, dragging myself, managed to touch the shackle and the tie. Both were in perfect order. I turned as quickly as possible to find the first place that would allow me to regain freedom. Phew! What a relief, fresh air! I sat down on a large block of ice with my boots in the water, my clothes soaking, panting a bit, yet bursting with happiness. A small reception committee was waiting where I had appeared from under the ice – six or seven gentoos who had probably done the same thing, walking carefully and skilfully under the ice, always near the largest supporting stones, so that they wouldn't, in a moment of bad luck, be crushed.

Without noticing that I was soaked to the skin, I spent almost an hour there, watching the small gentoos going about their magical, ceaseless business. After the sun's return in August, these elegant little animals had set aside their wandering winter existence and, settling in the nearby hills, had begun to pair off. This was the courtship period, during which both new and established couples would choose their nesting sites. For weeks they would go through an endless exchange of deliveries, and courtesies, and, alternatively, would go out on missions whose purpose, at first, I could not understand. They were looking for holes in the ice, not to fish but to bring back small pebbles. Finding pebbles was difficult, there were few spots not covered by ice or snow. The male would return after some hours, and place a small stone at his mate's feet (or vice-versa, because it wasn't easy to tell which was which). The other animal would express its gratitude with a guttural squawk, small wings stretched backwards, and then would be off, his or her turn to find another pebble in this non-stop relay. With these stones they would build nests for the eggs they would lay in October–November. At the end of the day, a couple would have gathered no more than a dozen pebbles. Older and more experienced couples chose spots protected from the wind and from the thaw, and would never abandon their small stock of stones. Younger, more passionate couples sometimes went off together in search of pebbles. When they came back they would find their neighbours had stolen the pebbles they'd left behind. They would then start up an appalling racket until some of the neighbours gave them back a handful of pebbles and the community could once again live in harmony.

For weeks, and then months, I followed their labours, as they brought their stones one by one, not stopping night or day. Sometimes a breeding pair chose a tilting shelf on which to build their nest and when they added one final stone to their pile, the whole lot would overbalance and roll down into the sea. Or the sun's heat would cause a piece of snow to fall, sweeping away weeks and weeks' worth of pebbles. Within seconds they would again start to gather new pebbles, in just the same place, and with the same patience. Many times I doubted that they would all manage to finish their nests. By the end, some nests would have more than 2,500 pebbles, the fruits of more than 2,500 journeys.

By September the penguin colony spreading over Damoy Point already had recognisable blocks and neighbourhoods. These creatures, at the same time so competitive, yet so dependent upon each other, had developed an incredible social architecture. The position of each nest followed rules that were both defensive and were for reasons of cohabitation. If the nests were positioned far apart, it would have allowed the skuas, predators of both eggs and chicks, to penetrate and attack. If the nests were sited too close together, one couple would inevitably start stealing its neighbour's pebbles. In the colony, the avenues down which the penguins waddled to gain access were a few centimetres wider. Yet if anyone chose to stop there they would receive shower of pecking. In a very short time, the value of small stones in the bay was sky-high.

Sometimes thicker, sometimes thinner, the snow would expose old hoards of pebbles used in previous seasons. I would always walk about with some in my pocket, sometimes I would rattle them in my hand and leave three or four between my boots. Immediately a small group would approach and then pause forty or fifty centimetres from my feet, looking at the stones. They'd stand there sizing up my height and exchanging looks, until finally a brave one would take the initiative and grab one of the stones, happily running away to his nest. Doubt, fear and courage – their behaviour patterns were not so different from those of humans. There were the little lapses, too. Theft, 'borrowing' and disappearance of pebbles; all failings which the gentoos seemed capable of pardoning with a wisdom that humans have not yet attained.

By the middle of October the days became longer than the nights. Barbara disappeared one Saturday and when she came back the following Monday she brought Horace, a furry pup who screamed continuously, and with whom I never got on very well. The best-built nest in the colony belonged to Theodore and Mariana, a pair of gentoos I recognised because Theodore had a cut above the left eye – probably due to an attack by a leopard seal. The first eggs appeared; most nests had two. One nest had three eggs, the work of Maria Amélia.

Finally, good weather, cold and sunny with the ice increasingly hard, which suggested *Paratii*'s freedom would come only in November or December.

And then, a terrible surprise. During a week of renewed high tides, the barometer suddenly dropped and Dorian Bay was seized by one of those storms that could no longer frighten me, coming up from the south-east. The ice in the Neumayer Channel didn't hold firm and piled up on one headland, opening a strip of free water right in front of the bay. The tide was incredibly high and though the entire Dorian Bay ice sheet didn't break, it detached itself from the surrounding rock and, with *Paratii* stuck in the middle, threatened to leave, carrying my boat right over the rocks at the entrance of the bay.

The mooring lines holding the boat, were now also holding the ice sheet covering the whole bay. If they broke, I was done for. If only the ice would break into pieces and flow out of the bay. But this wasn't going to happen. I put on my woolly hat, jumped from the boat on to the ice and ran nervously around it trying to find a solution. There wasn't one. We were heading for the rocks.

Horace, Barbara's pup, was screaming like a mad thing, making me even more nervous. Damnation. To be wrecked after all this time was the end. Despite all her strength, there wouldn't be much left of *Paratii* if she were pushed on to the rocks by the ice. I went out and came back six or seven times. All the cables were under the ice, and I didn't know what to do. Silently, his head and snout propped upon a stone, Theobald stared at me. But I couldn't just stand there with my arms folded.

My God! The chain-saw! The chain-saw in the hold.

I flew below decks, got the saw, which I'd never even started up, and holding the instruction book in front of me quickly put it together with my fingers shaking. It was topped up with fuel and had oil in the tank, the blade and chain were in position and so, still inside the boat, I started it. My God! What a noise this dangerous little device produced! But there was no time to worry. I threw a twenty-litre jerry-can of fuel on to the ice, along with two tins of oil for the chain and a small yellow funnel. Then I was off like a madman determined to cut the ice sheet into pieces, but at the same time worried about cutting the mooring ropes. When the first piece was starting to detach itself, I was 100 metres away from the fuel can, with one foot on either side of a cut that was gradually opening. To which side should I jump? How would I get back to the fuel again? And what would happen if the block of ice I chose to jump on floated away with me on it? A thousand decisions, all at the same time. I left the chain-saw, still running, on one side and ran to get the funnel and the fuel on the other. When I returned the ice was drifting away with the saw. I turned, ran and jumped. One foot landed on the water, but I landed flat on my knees and face on the other side. I started another long cut, my fingers aching, though not from the cold – it was −10°C and the wind was strong – but from having to press the throttle so hard. I went floating off on another piece with the machine in one hand, the can and the funnel on the other, but was just in time to leap right over to where Theobald sat, his mouth wide and eyes staring because of the racket I was making. Poor chap, he himself never made one single sound. I ran round the bay, over the rocks until I found a stone bridge that took me back to the biggest ice plate.

I stopped nine hours later after pouring in more fuel and more oil, and leaping from one piece of ice to the next like a madman. Nine hours covered with ice fragments that flew up from the chain all over my legs. My back ached and my ears were buzzing. But, one way or another, I had chopped the whole bay into pieces, some of them larger than a tennis court, and now they were piled up against the rocks. Just two ice-islands remained stuck to the mooring ropes, I would deal with them as soon as I launched *Vagabundo* next day.

Dear *Paratii* was safe, floating once again. Exhausted, I flung down the chain-saw in the cockpit after it had been turned off, and screamed. I screamed like a madman, with rage, with hate, with happiness. I screamed until I couldn't scream any more.

11

SEE YOU LATER, *RAPA NUI*!

I was sleeping like an angel lying on a soft bed of clouds when I was awoken by BANG, BANG, BANG. 'Oh my God! Not that ice again. It's too much! Never a minute's peace,' I grumbled and got up, still crumpled with sleep. Then I got a huge fright.

'How are you, man? Are you still alive?' Two human creatures right at my door! Pete Marquis was back.

The last human being I had seen the previous summer was the same one who almost killed me with shock now, seven and a half months later. It was the beginning of a new Antarctic season, and the British Antarctic Survey (BAS) ship, *John Biscoe*, was idling out there in the Neumayer Channel. Pete and his companion came over for five minutes, to say hello, have a cup of coffee and leave me a bag of fresh fruit. What great people. But soon they were off, their orange inflatable headed back to the ship which was ready to sail.

Summer again: hard to believe. And what a funny sensation to see someone you know as if only a weekend had gone by. It seemed as if the whole winter had passed more quickly than a rainy weekend. So, farewell polar darkness, endless walks under the moonlight, nights for serenading invisible girlfriends. Goodbye skiing competitions around

135

Paratii, visits to impossible glaciers, all part of that long weekend, now behind me.

A few days later, the same *John Biscoe* would return, and there would be plenty of visits, chats and stories. The BAS crew went to Rothera Base, in Marguerite Bay, and on to Fossil Bluff, 260 miles to the south. But my own calm and tranquillity would not return. It was time to leave. In a few weeks *Rapa Nui* would leave Brazil and we had planned to meet up, probably in Dorian Bay itself.

The inflatable was back in operation, working the same route as last summer. On the other hand, there was still a lot to do on board *Paratii*. The deck was covered in snow; there were frozen 'snakes' in the cockpit; and the radio antennae, which formed an inverted V, would have to be dismantled and the engine, the generator, batteries, electrics and all the instruments had to be overhauled. The Reflex heater was exchanged for the small one with the little inspection window.

All the nests had eggs. All of them. Not a single nest was unfinished out of almost 1,200, though I had doubted they would ever complete the task. Horace, heavier and clumsier each day, finally managed to bite my heel. The still-silent Theobald was making the best of the heat from the dark rocks that were gradually appearing from under the ice. Time was flying. And I would forget, every night, there was no longer any darkness and I would end up sleeping just when it was time to bake the bread in the Continental Bakery, now in business almost every day.

On the penultimate day of November, an unexpected visitor arrived as I was coming back from a successful scaling of the 'magic mountain', the gigantic iceberg which had been aground in the channel for months.

I had barely got inside when an infernal row broke the afternoon calm. Looking through the window, I couldn't believe it. Penguins flying! Flapping their wings down the hill, running over the stones and over each other in panic and despair. Chaos! A large helicopter had appeared from nowhere and was crossing Damoy Point at the end of the bay, flying low right over the penguin rookery. An idiotic Argentine military helicopter, aircraft number 2H238, had flown in from far away – perhaps Paradise Bay or the Gerlache Strait – and could easily have avoided the nests and landed 200 metres earlier. A group of ten or twelve strange creatures, decked out with epaulettes and cameras, emerged from the aircraft, which, as though its mere presence had not caused enough havoc, carried out two more landings and take-offs to inspect a shelter flying the Argentine flag that the English used as a lavatory. What stupidities these desk-bound geo-politicians commit when they rashly stick their flags in the wrong places.

The gentoos, terrified, abandoned the nests, built over months of endless pebble-collection; while the delighted skuas attacked the nests, breaking or carrying off eggs on all sides. A week later one could still see hundreds of broken eggshells resting on the bottom of the bay's crystal-clear waters. It was my saddest week in Antarctica, although December has been the most beautiful and calmest month. Many of the gentoos, when they returned, would try to brood these broken eggs, sitting on lifeless nests. Other couples remained on their nests right until the end of the season, as male and female took turns to brood non-existent eggs or care for imaginary chicks, while their neighbours fed the small survivors.

During a long communication with Brazil I spoke via radio-telephone hook-up to a great university friend, Bráulio Pasmanik. It was his birthday and he was determined to get to the bottom of the story about this Barbara, and why I was no longer living alone. I also heard during this transmission that *Rapa Nui* had been delayed and would not arrive in time to spend Christmas with me. I also spoke to my father, his voice so angry and emotional as he delivered quotations in

Arabic, that I could almost see his huge side-whiskers and penetrating gaze.

On 15 December the first gentoo chicks of Dorian Bay were born. New inhabitants on the planet. The first to emerge from his egg was given the name Germanito and he was a neighbour of Mariana and Theodore, some ten nests away. On the following day it was time for *Rapa Nui* to break out and leave its own nest – Brazil. At this point I was just as nervous as those on board, but our long-hoped-for rendezvous would now only be possible during the second half of January, too late to travel south to visit the BAS people in Marguerite Bay. There was still ice around Renaud Island, making the passage south complicated.

I was dying to get away, to see my red boat reborn, and to see if after eleven months of idleness everything would work again. I decided to wait one more week and try to get down to Marguerite Bay in time to meet up with *Rapa Nui* on my return.

On midsummer day, the old laundry on the rocks was back in business, although it was still half-covered. Clean, dry clothes, everything checked and ready. The morning was a little colder, −2°C or −3°C, the sea was so calm and clear that a plate of glassy ice, two centimetres thick, covered the bay. I began the job of removing all the mooring lines.

I had expected so much of this day, the moment of pulling in the lines and departing. On so many occasions my journey and that of *Paratii* had depended on those ropes. They had been manufactured with great care and efficiency by a rope-maker from southern Brazil called São Leopoldo. After a year of continuous labour – high tension, abrasion, sun and razor-sharp ice – not even a single thread was broken. The ropes were as intact and supple as on the first day.

As the outboard motor had already been stowed away,

I went over to the rocks rowing *Vagabundo*, breaking the frozen surface of the waters with the oar I had brought from Paraty. I worked quickly. The tide was half-way in and I didn't have any problem releasing the ropes from the 'flat rock' and from 'south rock'. When I arrived at the safety anchor on the north-eastern rocks, it lay in a metre and a half of water and despite several attempts I couldn't release it. There was no one to help me and I wasn't prepared to wait for the tide to go down. Without stopping to think, I broke open a larger hole in the ice with my oar and then – wearing overalls, sweater and boots – took a breath and dived in, seized the fifty-kilo anchor, threw it in the boat and rowed like mad for home, to change my clothes. It all happened so quickly I didn't have time to feel cold. Soon afterwards, dried out, my hair combed and my heart beating strongly, I switched on the engine and the main anchor windlass. The chain was hauled in, the anchor fitted into its place on the pulpit with a snap and slowly *Paratii* made her way out of Dorian Bay.

I was leaving behind almost a year of my life in this place. A beautiful and busy year, during which I learned more about people and more about the world than in all the other trips I had undertaken. A private year I would never forget.

Many pups were born in this last week. Barbara left for good and I lost track of Horace. There was a crystalline silence as *Paratii* made her way to the mouth of the bay, gently breaking the thin sheet of ice. The only mammal remaining on land was the same shy, quiet sea-elephant. I still don't know why, or how, but just at the moment I passed between the rocks at the bay's entrance, Theobald, who had never let out a single sound, lifted his head and began to scream. I screamed back and he didn't stop. He screamed without stopping as I passed Casabianca Island, screaming at the top of his voice, maybe with joy, maybe not, the sole occupier of Dorian

139

Bay. The last sounds I heard from Dorian Bay were his screams.

*   *   *

On Christmas Eve I stopped at Palmer Station, where I finally met Ajo and four of the funniest people I'd ever met in my life: Mary Franklin, a beautiful blonde body-builder from Alaska; Dr Farouk, a Pakistani from Cripps Institute in California; the base doctor, Matt; and a PhD in glaciology who almost collapsed from laughing too much. It was a beautiful stop, during which I almost destroyed my boat or rather Florence the wind vane. Manoeuvring *Paratii* in front of the base, I crashed the stern violently into an iceberg that had shot quickly through the narrow channel. A bit of the monster broke off and got stuck in the tubular structure which protected the rudder. Despite the enormous crash, nothing else happened. If it had not been for the massive structure designed by Jean on one of his inspired days, I wouldn't have been left with even the shadow of my rudder as a souvenir. Having witnessed my scandalous performance, Dr Farouk was visibly concerned about my sailing skills.

I also managed to get in contact with Pete Marquis and Alan, or Mr Osborne as he was called at Rothera Base. 'Brrilliant, Colonel Klink! Brrilliant! Everything's fine here in Marguerite Bay! When are you coming, Amyr?' He would always joke in his funny Scottish accent.

There was still ice obstructing the way south. On New Year's Day I stopped on Hovegaard Island, where Hugo had been experiencing difficulties. His boat *Oviri* was still stuck in the ice, and he had to wait several more weeks before he could free himself. To the north of Pleneau Island at the entrance of the beautiful and impressive Le Maire Channel, I visited another gentoo-penguin colony. I named it 'Apocalypse Rookery' – because of the stunning beauty of the place and because of the drama that was taking place there.

An enormous family of sea-elephants had installed themselves amongst the nests. Some of these nests still had gentoo eggs in them. Normally Theobald's relatives are not aggressive and don't attack penguins, but their brutal and heavy movements can often carry away whole nests without them noticing. The small penguins were not intimidated and didn't run away until the last second. They would sit on their eggs and protect their chicks, pecking and shrieking in protest against three or four tons of deaf sea-elephant. There wasn't much I could do. Seeing so many nests being destroyed and couples staying together reminded me of the Argentine helicopter.

On 9 January I was going southward in the direction of Crystal Sound, electric with happiness and expectation. What a diabolically beautiful part of the world. And what joy to feel *Paratii* behaving perfectly, absolutely perfectly, casting the shadow of her sails over icebergs of the most incredible colours. I wasn't sure whether I should stop or go straight on to Adelaide Island. I needed some sleep and, for the first time, I couldn't leave the boat in the hands of the automatic pilot. Every moment I had to avoid big bergs or slacken sail to cross a field of brash ice. I was sailing with sail and motor together, in case there was the need for an emergency manoeuvre.

My doubts were gone in seconds. Despite the clear sunshine the clouds darkened as in a horror film. At six degrees above zero, it began to pour. Real rain, with fog as thick as cotton-wool and a 35-knot north-east wind. Oh joy! What more terrible conditions could I wish for? But I saved my reputation following the disastrous manoeuvre at Palmer: I sailed beautifully through the channel leading into Mutton Cove, a tiny island with a natural stone quay only a bit longer than a boat. Without cracking one single egg I moored in a perfect manoeuvre that, unfortunately, no one saw.

Tying up a boat without being able to make mistakes or to turn back because of strong winds and with no one to throw the mooring rope to, is not easy. Nor, of course, were there any ready-made places to tie up to. But little by little I developed a technique and became skilled with my ropes, chains and inflatable. Quite quickly I was able to moor *Paratii* in seconds, long before she could sail away with no one aboard. The rope rolls capable of paying out up to 200 metres of rope were more useful than a dozen creaky sailors in these situations.

That same day I had a fantastic talk by radio with Hermann on board *Rapa Nui*. On board too were Eduardo 'The Flyer' Fausto and the incredible Professor Villela. This must have been at least his twentieth trip to Antarctica. Their position at 19:50 GMT was 50° 32′ south, 65° 59′ west. So they really were on their way, just entering the *screaming fifties*, right in the heart of albatross country, and they were surrounded by dozens of them. Another fifteen degrees of latitude and if all went well, we would soon be seeing each other.

On the fourth rainy day at Mutton Cove, I was suddenly blown off the rock I was tied up to. The wind went round to the south and the tiny, narrow bay filled up with huge pieces of ice. I didn't have time to finish my breakfast. I jumped on to the rocks, loosed all the ropes from the top of the island in just enough time to get back to the boat and then set off under full throttle before I got stuck in the bay. With a southerly wind, Mutton Cove is a real mousetrap. Then, as a reward for my initiative, the sun came out and the wind came blowing sweetly from the north-east, favouring my descent of the peninsula. Delirious joy!

Twenty-seven hours and forty-five minutes later, sailing non-stop, around endless ice pieces, almost no time to

142

make coffee, I anchored at Lagoon Island, in perfect weather.

Immediately after crossing the Antarctic Circle I passed a festival of whales – humpback, I think – a true spectacle among pieces of shiny 'prismatic' ice I'd never seen before. Marguerite Bay, immense and beautiful, was named in 1909 in honour of Meg, his beloved second wife, by Jean B. Charcot, who came there aboard his beautiful three-master *Pourquoi Pas?*. His first wife had divorced him, claiming desertion during his first Antarctic winter sojourn in 1904–5, aboard *Le Français*.

The Gullet, the narrow channel that leads into the bay and separates Adelaide Island from the continent, was blocked, so I entered Marguerite Bay around the outside of the big island. Despite the size of Marguerite Bay, there are not as many anchorages as one would imagine from looking at the chart. What one does find, quite different from much of the rest of the Antarctic Peninsula, is a broad, expansive natural beauty, where a boat will feel neither hedged in nor imprisoned. Space all around us, sun shining both night and day, *Paratii* was a guest of magnificent Marguerite Bay, in a week of what seemed like eternal peace.

And thanks to one tiny detail, this week almost turned out to be eternal. On the southern side of Lagoon Island I discovered a small pool of thawed ice which was ideal as water for the never-ending laundry. I'd just had another contact with *Rapa Nui*: Eduardo had given his new position as latitude 60° 48′ south, longitude 64° 16′ west. For God's sake! This meant they were in the middle of the Drake Passage, less than 300 miles from Dorian Bay. So both yachts were now about the same distance from my winter bay. As communication was very poor, Eduardo asked for another radio link-up in forty-five minutes. I agreed, but for some reason was restless and decided to use those forty-five minutes to tackle the business of the fresh water and clothes. I jumped into the tender with two buckets, started the motor and was flying off in the direction of the pool of fresh water when I remembered the anchor. My God! I'd forgotten the anchor! If I were to go back now I wouldn't have time. So I went on and, instead of leaving the boat on the little beach and walking across the island, I went by sea, around the island, to save time.

I had hardly begun my washing when a dark shadow appeared in the sky and the wind came up. 'Better forget the clothes and get home, there's a wind coming!' I ran back to *Vagabundo*, and untied it while the wind was hurling the sea against the rocks. I was in an open space, but encircled by jagged rocks and there was no space to push the boat away and put the outboard in the water to start her up. I lost precious minutes and when I was finally far enough out to start the motor, the propeller struck a rock and, ZAP! lost the propeller pin. Oh my God! I was drifting, my oars unable to compete with the wind and the waves. There was one last rock a little further on, where I sheltered to avoid being swept away by the ever-increasing wind. I had to jump into the water up to my waist to hold her steady. Holding on to the inflatable with one hand, I opened the outboard engine cover, took out the plastic bag containing the tools and grabbed one of the spare propeller pins. There were three of them. I don't know how I managed it, but while holding on to a boat that was leaping over the small waves, I changed the propeller pin, put everything quickly away, jumped inside and started the engine. It caught on the first pull, and then ZAP! we struck another rock and the propeller pin broke again. Oh no! This was not funny any more. I managed to get to the very last rock at the end of the island, rowing like mad. If I had failed to reach it this time I would have been a goner. There was nowhere to stand in the water, and with shaking fingers I changed the second propeller pin. This time it had to work. As I was putting the propeller back, the cotter pin broke. I had one last spare cotter pin, and I fixed it, again waist-high in water, hanging on to the boat for dear life. Pulling away for the third time, unable to see the rocks for the waves, about twenty metres out, unbelievably, I hit another rock, and the retaining pin broke again. Now it was panic. I took a deep breath and did nothing. There was only one pin left in the plastic bag – the one I had made and nearly thrown away in the winter. I was in a kind of circle of submerged rocks and had to get away. I drifted off, leaving the island quickly. *Paratii* wasn't far, 300 metres perhaps. But against the wind, it was impossible to reach her. With all the calm I could muster, I raised the motor and dismantled the propeller for the third time, keeping the pin between my teeth, for fear of losing it and because my fingers were aching with cold. If I dropped this pin in the water, it was goodbye. The last pin. I assembled everything, leaping like a goat on top of the waves and closed the cotter pin very, very carefully. The island was more and more distant. Now, even if I had a hundred metres of rope and an anchor, there was no stopping the drift. I pulled the starter rope. The second pull started it. I accelerated slowly, not towards the island, but around it. This place was a nest of vipers; a place the charts call 'unsurveyed'.

With my right hand on the throttle I headed into the wind, spray from the wavetops hitting me in the face. I remained stiff and motionless, not because of the cold, but with sheer tension, until I was able to lay my hands on *Paratii*'s deck. Ten minutes later, drying myself out by the side of the heater, I heard Eduardo and Hermann calling on the radio. It had been a very close call.

Our great rendezvous was to take place in Dorian Bay and so as soon as the weather cleared a bit, I planned to go up there and meet them. The sun returned that evening, but both Anchorage and Lagoon Islands were encircled by a thick layer of ice – sheet ice, growlers, icebergs, bergy bits, the lot – so I spent two days with my boat imprisoned. Mad with tension, I tried to pass the time by practising knots as *Paratii* placidly drifted with the ice, I knew that by then *Rapa Nui* would already be in Dorian Bay, waiting for me.

This test of nerves was worth while, and when I'd escaped the ice, the sun shone and a 25-knot southerly blew. I left Marguerite Bay at high speed, under sail, motor, and, if I could have done, with paddles and oars as well. It was a perfect trip, no stops or problems, but it meant sailing for forty-one hours without closing my eyes. It was three o'clock in the morning when I rounded Damoy Point into Dorian Bay. What a blow! There was no *Rapa Nui* waiting for me. Downcast, I anchored without even fixing the mooring ropes around the rocks, and slept.

Close by was a very famous Swedish yacht, *Northern Light*. It belonged to Rolph and Deborah, a couple whose book, an impressive photographic work, was with me on board, and which had inspired my wish to visit Moffen Island, a spectacular spot in the Arctic. Next morning I chatted with the crew of the Swedish boat before they left. They planned to spend the winter in a yet-to-be-chosen spot. But I could see no blue schooner. At 18:00 local time, just as *Northern Light* was leaving, I heard Hermann on the radio. As they had not found me in Dorian Bay when they first arrived, they had gone on to Paradise Bay, but they were already on their way back.

By 22:00 I was getting really impatient, going up and down the mast with my binoculars to scan the horizon almost non-stop. At last, I saw a blue hull with two masts. It's them! My God! It's them! I was jumping with happiness on the deck.

What a great day. And what a celebration we were anticipating. One year and twenty-three days after our last encounter in Jurumirim! What a party this was going to be!

Such emotion! There were only some minutes to go. But Fate works in mysterious ways. No one could say the weather was good. Grey skies and a 25-knot north-east wind which forces boats in there at full speed: the worst weather for entering the bay. I had all my instruments turned on and could see the needle of the wind-speed indicator steadily rising to thirty knots, and gusting thirty-five. Suddenly it leapt to forty, to forty-five, and then was gusting to fifty knots. 'For God's sake, it's impossible blowing like this,' I thought. My cat's cradle of mooring ropes was occupying half the bay as it stretched from one side of the rocks to the other. Under normal conditions I'd have expected them to moor alongside me on the lee side. But in this wind it was impossible. They would have to cast anchor with no space for manoeuvres.

I was watching everything through my binoculars. I could see the blue boat approaching, past the dead glaciers on their right, ready to come in. They were flying, everyone on deck. This, as Eduardo would say, was turning out to be a 'radical' manoeuvre.

To complicate things further, there were huge pieces of ice coming into the bay or crossing its mouth. *Rapa Nui* entered, turned towards me and came up into the wind a few metres from where I was. 'Ready? Ready! Let go!' Hermann released the anchor chain and someone yelled, 'Too soon.' Someone else screamed, 'Abort!' The anchor came up and went down again, Hermann jumped in the inflatable with a hundred metres of rope and a second anchor and went off at high speed to the rocks to tie up. I was watching everything from on deck, leaning over the rail of *Paratii*, screaming over the high wind.

'The rope is tangled up at the bow!'

'What?'

'There's a knot! The rope won't go through! Look out astern!'

'What?'

147

'Astern, you're going to crash. The fenders. Where are the fenders! Where are the fenders? That's it. No, bring the bigger rope. Quick, the other rope! Can't you see it? That one! Right! Hold on there! Hold on there . . .'

The wind was blowing strongly, whistling through the rigging with the halyards on all three masts banging noisily and the snow coming down horizontally, everyone running, pulling . . .

'Now! Release it! Looser! Quick! The other end!' Half an hour with everyone yelling at the tops of their voices. Little by little these two old aluminium friends, one blue, the other red, approached and finally touched each other. We tied up all the ropes leaping from one to the other, panting because of so much shouting. Then Hermann stopped in front of me, soaking wet, his hair full of snow:

'Look here, you son of a bitch! Good afternoon!'

We punched each other on the breast, then had a long hug and finally everyone began to laugh and jump about. What a tumultuous arrival, but what a party! It was 22:30 hours on 23 January.

Letters, news, presents, orders, constant to-ings and fro-ings from one boat to the other, endless chats. During those first days I couldn't sleep, such was my happiness at seeing the old crew again, at getting news from home and even at seeing a newspaper with classified advertisements, only a month old.

There was no good weather or easy winds during those days; it snowed almost constantly, interrupted by gusts of wind. Despite this, these were ten days of tense and nervous joy, the best moments of the whole trip, perhaps the best ten days of my life. *Paratii* received new life as we transferred a good part of the winter supplies to *Rapa Nui*, to be taken back to Brazil. In exchange, I got new tapes, records and books. We also swapped nautical maps and charts; these would be needed by those on board *Rapa Nui*: they were planning to cruise further down in these

The chain and cables
disappear into the ice
while neighbours like this
sheathbill approach
(*above*).

A pair of *Pygoscelis papua* continuously share all the tasks – from searching for pebbles to build the nest to feeding the chicks that hatch in November–December.

The chief predators come either from
the sea – the leopard-seal – or from
the sky – the skuas. On land, not
even the size of a sea-lion will force
the gentoos to abandon their nests.

A turbulent and noisy existence, in which problems with the neighbours are interrupted by unexpected visitors.

One year after the departure from Jurumirim
the encounter in Antarctica we have all dreamed about: ter
days alongside the blue schooner. Some hours after thi
photo was taken, *Paratii* sailed off for the Arctic

Barbara the Weddell seal, my
faithful companion through the
winter. She gave birth to Horace
and only left when the ice melted.

Dorian Bay, freed,
illuminated by the
lingering summer sun.

Or motionless, bathed in ▶
'winter sun': a full moon
nearly as clear as day.

Moffen Island, a ring of precious stones north of Spitsbergen. *Paratii* sailed 19,000 miles for a three-hour landfall here.

In front of the three crowns of
Kungsfjord, the encounter with
Arctic ice. From here Roald Amundsen
left for his first Arctic crossing, on
board the Zeppelin *Norge*.

After reflecting her image on waters at two extremes of the planet, and after sailing 27,000 miles in twenty-two months, *Paratii* returns to the exact point of departure: Jurumirim.

parts. On Saturday 2 February we swapped over positions so that my boat was now on the outside of the ropes and ready to go, secured to *Rapa Nui* by a single cable. We took a photo of all five of us on deck with the automatic shutter. And then another, just in case. I felt a dry knot in my throat, the one we feel when the time has come.

'Hermann, cast off the rope over there. Have a good journey, you people! See you in Brazil!'

'*Bon voyage*, Amyr!' Then *Rapa Nui* blew her siren until I vanished behind Casabianca Island.

'Farewell to all the animals of Dorian Bay. I'll see you some day.'

In front of me lay another 25,000 nautical miles before I'd hear that siren again.

12

THE GREEN FLASH

I nstalled in the cockpit, I was thinking about those penguin pebbles. How many pebbles would I give to calm this howling wind?

While completing the course on marine diesel engines at Perkins in England, I had been given a handy carry-all bag which had been hanging around, though I'd never found a use for it.

A few hours before leaving Antarctica, while ashore with Eduardo releasing *Paratii*'s mooring ropes, I found an abandoned penguin's nest and counted its pebbles. There were more than 2,000. By chance, the carry-all was in the inflatable and I couldn't resist putting a handful of them into the bag. Every time I opened the bag the smell of gentoos invaded the cabin, a funny smell that I learned to like. Now, without much to do, except keep a look-out as we sailed along, I spent hours tying knots, using a small pebble as the core of a 'monkey's fist' – a knot frequently used on board yachts – and then hung them on the wheel.

Sailing against the weather, neither hungry nor tired, I just watched the spectacle around me. The mainsail reefed to the maximum against the fifty-knot east-north-easterly, I skimmed along at a speed of more than ten knots. From time to time icebergs appearing in the distance would command my attention. Despite huge winds, *Paratii* behaved with class and elegance, flying along like an albatross. Wind-blown spray from the waves broke over the bows and the gunwales, turning to ice on the deck. This was hardly the weather or the wind I had hoped for as I took leave of Antarctica to enter the Drake Passage; but, quiet and tense, tying knots without ceasing, I felt a certain pleasure. In earlier days in the tropics, with winds far weaker than these, I would have been in terrible trouble. But now, with the sails trimmed and well under control after the last reefing, *Paratii* was again a true sailing yacht, on her most exhuberant form. The automatic pilot was working perfectly and with every wave the bows hurled up impressive showers of spray.

The most amazing thing was that the sea didn't look threatening, despite the swell. There were big waves, huge waves, but regular ones topped with foam, moved by a strong, constant wind that blew rather than gusted. If the weather did not get worse, I'd have no reason to worry. But if the wind increased, I'd have to go out on deck again to take down the mainsail and put up the small triangular stormsail. Fully dressed for work on deck, with boots, gloves and safety harness, I kept an eye on both the wind indicator and the sails. At 22:00 GMT the anemometer needle went beyond fifty-five knots. 'We can't wait any longer. Let's take in more sail.' But there was a layer of ice covering the mast and the groove in which the sail was held. No power on earth could get a sail down from a frozen mast. I climbed up the mast a couple of metres, hanging on to the first steps and supporting myself on the sail. Then I discovered just why it had been so important to insist on a black-coloured mast. When I touched the ice, it fell away like an ice lolly dropping from its stick. I climbed up to the first spreader and seconds later there was no ice on the dark surface of the mast. All the metalwork that had not been anodised in black remained ice-covered. I got the sail down, tied it up as I best could and, in its place, put up the storm triangle. In less than five minutes, I was back in the comfort of my cockpit.

That storm in the Drake Passage lasted for two days, but by the end of the third day I had practically crossed the whole strait. After reaching the latitude of Cape Horn – 56° south – *Paratii* would face only light breezes on her way to the Cape of Good Hope. I had never sailed in such heavy seas before; on the second day the wind reached almost seventy knots. On the other hand I could never have imagined it would be possible to make such a civilised crossing under these circumstances. I went out on the deck three times only and, after trimming the sails and setting my course, I had no need to alter anything else.

Paratii never once lost control in those waves as she rode up almost vertical walls of dark water, and went surfing down the other side. The build-up of ice didn't get any worse, and slowly, the chill I felt in my stomach at each wave, simply turned into hunger. It was hard to imagine that in a short time I would find myself desperately missing those two days.

Some way to the east of Cape Horn, an unexpected flat calm settled on the South Atlantic. The spot famous for its mountainous seas and furious winds was absolutely still and quiet.

By travelling a few degrees northward a distinct world had materialised. The water temperature increased, nights became darker and well-defined, and albatrosses once again kept me company. Now we had a problem in common: the total lack of wind. The insignificant breezes that did blow came from the north-east – precisely where I was heading – and failed even to fill the sails. My neighbours the albatrosses were grumpily getting on with life as best they could, swimming around like ducks on a pond. I could have turned on the motor, but since I was still 4,000 nautical miles from Africa, this didn't make a lot of sense.

By this time *Rapa Nui* had left Antarctica, heading for the Beagle Channel. On 11 February, just as I was in the middle of cooking up a pan of popcorn in the galley, Hermann came across on our 'Drake' radio frequency. Oddly, all he would say about their progress was that they were getting along 'more or less all right' and that they were 100 miles from Cape Horn. I was well to the east of the Falklands, a long way from them, becalmed. I had listened to the weather bulletin on Radio Magellan and I knew that near the Cape things were supposed to be pretty awful.

The next day I found out exactly how bad they were. *Rapa Nui* had been caught squarely in a deep weather depression coming in from the Pacific. Amongst the high seas and strong winds came a rogue wave, and she was capsized. For the first time in her life, the blue schooner put both her masts down into the water. Though little damage was done, everyone on board was very alarmed, even though they were just eight miles from the Cape and then the sheltered waters of the Beagle Channel.

The radar unit mounted on the mast filled with water, and the hard top for the main hatch was ripped off. But the hardest hit were Fausto and Professor Villela. The distinguished professor was hit by a bottle of chilli peppers that flew across the galley. I know it wasn't funny at the time, but given his pathological aversion for chilli pepper and his penguin-like movements, it was impossible not to laugh on hearing of the misfortune.

For anyone coming from Antarctica, travelling northward just a few degrees brings a special emotion. Each day becomes a little warmer, each day another item of clothing is discarded, until finally one can sit in the sun bare-chested. Pipes and hoses are flexible once again, in the mornings the honey is no longer solid – even the toothpaste comes out of the tube properly and lunch can be served on the 'terrace' – small pleasures that become sacred at each new spot on the map.

My route, however, crossed just north of South Georgia Island and to the south of Tristan da Cunha, travelling right down the central path of the westerlies. At these latitudes, famous and constant winds blow their way right around the planet. But something strange was happening, ever since that storm in the Drake Passage I had found no trace of the westerlies. There was a short, choppy swell, with light winds from all different directions, interspersed with endless periods of flat calm. Every two days, one day would be spent motionless. Frequently I would find that during a 24-hour period I had made less progress than if I had been rowing a small dinghy across the Atlantic.

Distracted, fiddling about behind the main radio looking for a pair of dividers, I saw a white dot on the horizon out of the corner of my eye. When I got hold of the dividers, and raised my head, I got a rude shock. A ship, Korean or Chinese, *Ching I N.137*, was bearing down on me. I ran to the radio and called VHF, channel 16, nothing. I dashed to Florence, and took over the helm myself. A rusty fishing boat with thirty-odd crew, bobbing about like a truck on its last legs, had come over just to take a look. A hard, lonely life those fishermen lead; month after month beyond sight of land and with no fixed course, simply wandering around in search of shoals of fish. Despite the choppy sea, and with sails up and little wind, my boat was infinitely more stable than theirs.

A shameful effort: 49.2 miles in twenty-four hours. I discovered that frequently, a calm sea can do more damage than a healthy squall. There was not enough wind to fill the sails. Rocking from side to side, listening to the battens in the mainsail banging and the saucepans rattling in the galley, it was difficult to sleep or to stay in a good mood. A ghostly fog engulfed *Paratii* and I had the worst kind of accident. I went on deck barefoot, stubbed my toe on a winch and – exquisite agony – lifted off a toe-nail. An arsenal of curses exploded in every direction. And, as if the heavens had heard my imprecations in the middle of the afternoon of that irritating last day in February, the mist lifted, the sun took over and a spectacular sunset ensued.

Since childhood, I have had this desire, difficult to realise, expecially in Brazil, whose coastline faces the rising sun, that wherever I was, I would search out a sunset over the sea. I was searching for that rare phenomenon, mentioned by nearly all sailors in the past: the green flash. A ray of light, or a light explosion, which takes place in special conditions at the exact moment when the last splinter of sun goes over the horizon.

I quickly put some plaster on my toe, carefully put on my tennis shoes, ran back to the stern of *Paratii* and climbed on the bar where the radar antenna was fitted, where I used to sit while making astronomical observations. I was carrying out the usual ritual without any expectation that this day would be any different. 'Nineteen hundred hours, fifty-five minutes and thirty seconds . . . forty seconds . . . fifty . . . there it goes . . . the sun . . . Goodbye . . .' Then I yelled: 'I saw it! I saw it! I saw it! The rascal, I saw it!' Such a long time and I had finally seen it: the green flash! A fraction of second that was worth the whole journey.

My map of the South Atlantic was being steadily crossed by a long pencilled arc pointing to South Africa. As each day passed, the white space in front of that line – the distance still to be travelled – was reduced by a new position. What a struggle! There were no problems, strong winds or heavy seas. Far worse, periods of calm succeeded periods of calm. Light, hesitant winds blew from all directions but that which the *South Atlantic Pilot* promised was the prevailing direction. Every day I would face westward and sing a song composed by the Brazilian musician Dorival Caymmi: 'Let's summon the wind, eh, Curimã . . .' Nothing. And then, so as not to keep on hearing the hollow sound of the empty sails flapping, I'd play a very funny tape, by a Breton group called Soldat Louis: songs of Breton sailors, their whore-houses and their sufferings in the high seas.

Du rhum, des femmes et d'la bière nom de Dieu . . .
Un accordéon pour valser tant qu'on veut
Du rhum, des femmes, c'est ça qui rend heureux
Que l'diable nous emporte, on a rien trouvé d'mieux . . .

Another 1,500 miles to the Cape. When, oh when, Good Hope? Just a year ago I had leapt off *Paratii* wearing my skis, walking across solid sea, so far back in the past now, I could hardly believe it. Months that had flown like light, one after another. And now I was struggling against a calm that made every hour of the day seem like an eternity, the only dream I had was that of arriving. I desperately wanted to arrive, and time would not move. Less than twelve days to Cape Town, twelve positions to be plotted on the map, and they weighed as much as a whole year. In fact I wasn't just crossing the Atlantic, I was crossing two Atlantics, four seasons and a whole existence that lasted for fifteen months.

It was exactly fifteen months and two days since I had seen any tree or bush. Fifteen months since I had left Joatinga Point in Paraty. A supermarket, a town, a traffic jam, a wood, nothing.

On 3 March Serge Gainsbourg – some of whose writings and songs, such as 'J'aimerais mourir vivant', I had on board – died. Time, finally, never stops. And during those fifteen months many things had happened in the world. The Berlin Wall had fallen. Those trees I had planted in São Paulo just before my departure, one stormy day when I had decided to throw away all my bureaucratic and civilian responsibilities, had grown and flowered. There had been another war in the Middle East. Despite being physically distant from the world in which things were happening and trees continued growing, I knew that not a second of these fifteen months had been lost.

On 14 March, after forty-one days at sea, I plotted another point on my chart. A hundred and sixty-four miles until I reached the cape founded by Bartholomew Días. Less than twenty-four hours till land appeared again. Used to the flat calms, I had a bath, a shave and cut my hair. I took on as decent and civilised a look as I could and prepared the boat for a peaceful landfall in Table Bay. Cape Town, one of the most beautiful harbours in the world. I was even making plans. What had become of friends I had left in so complex a country?

Approaching land is always a tense business, especially in a spot such as the Cape. Ships from all over the world in transit between the Atlantic and Indian Oceans, come close to the Cape. Any sailing boat going through this corridor needs to take as much care as one would need to push a supermarket trolley across a motorway. A breeze came up. Then it really began to blow, as if to remind me that a voyage doesn't end just anywhere, but at a precise place, chosen and achieved. Until you reach this place, there's no true arrival.

The last position: seventy-seven miles from the coast. Ship ahoy! Coming from the Indian Ocean, with no clear direction, I watched it through my binoculars and on the radar. Rather than risk anything, I went about and waited for it to pass. It was only then that I realised that neither the wind nor the waves were fooling. In these short, choppy seas another ship appeared. Mother of God! Another one. I tuned to channel 16 on the radio and heard Cape Town Radio. African voices, transmitting from a safe, secure base on land; but the weather news was really bad. The forecast was for force 10–11 winds, or 45–55 knots, gusting 60, between Cape Agulhas and the Cape of Good Hope. I hadn't experienced such weather since the southern Drake Passage, centuries ago.

Nor could I see land. Had I missed Africa? Then at 16:02 GMT a shadow appeared before my bows. I gulped. There it was. I could see the Cape of Good Hope, once known as the Cape of Storms, now under storm. The sky darkened and the sea became truly angry, while ship after ship came by. I sailed north with a strong south-easterly wind, trying to surf down the waves at a better angle. In the darkness, I trimmed the sail badly and the ultra-violet protection strip was shredded off by the wind and began to make a terrible noise. Before it got tangled in something serious, I rolled up the sail and tried to cut the strip off, but it was too high up.

Another ship, and a rapid change of course. My God, what traffic! Better to turn on the engine. I turned the ignition, but for the first time in its life the motor wouldn't take. Nervously I kept turning the key, but nothing. Of course! There must be air in the diesel-fuel system. Worried about the ships that were passing by like trains and distracted by the non-stop flapping of the white strip, I was anxious to get back up on deck. I grabbed the toolbox but, just as I was starting to work on the fuel pipe, the box slipped, crushing an oil can and sending oil-bespattered tools flying in all directions. The bilges were filling up with a soup of Mobil Formula One oil mixed with tools, as I tried to turn the engine again. Nothing. It's very easy to lose patience under such circumstances, so I slopped my oily way to the galley to make myself a glass of passion-fruit drink. I put the glass down on the bench and breathed deeply before shouting a curse. The glass went flying, with juice and spoon, against the wall. *Paratii* was listing violently from side to side as I restarted the juice-making operation – but this time in an unbreakable glass. I concentrated again on the motor: I unblocked the airlock, mustering all the calm I could in such a situation, and this time it worked. Lights on the coastal slopes; little flashing lights, cars perhaps. I went flying on the wind into the bay in front of the city, while the spray blew off the little waves, drenching the hull and getting into my eyes. A tug coming out between the two moles left no space for a second vessel, and forced me to turn about, so I had to come back in all over again. Where on earth could I stop in such a wind? I went past Duncan Docks under power, all the sails down, motoring past huge moored ships that groaned and whined as they were pushed against the dockside fenders by a wind which made *Paratii* heel right over.

It was one o'clock in the morning and I was surrounded by ghost ships, no one to help with a rope. There beyond the last ship – a Korean fishing boat – was the yacht harbour and a buoy for visitors. But how was I to pick up a heavy buoy on my own? How could I thread my mooring rope and manoeuvre the boat at the same time, without *Paratii*'s twenty-five tons destroying a dozen fibreglass sailing boats that were tied up all around? A deafening noise of wind whistling through hundreds of masts, cables, and halyards banging as frenetically as thousands of bells. I made three acrobatic attempts, three fantastic tries, running along the deck with the engine accelerating but with no one at the helm, while I tried to hang over the bows to hook up to the buoy. But I did it on the fourth attempt. In those last twenty-four hours I had worked harder, and caused more chaos and disorder than during the entire voyage, the Drake Passage included. But it was worth it: during that same night, I stepped on to dry land in a real port, took off my boots and my socks and felt the grass beneath my bare feet. Grass that was greener than the green flash.

13

UNCROSSABLE CAPES

S itting on deck watching the traffic go by, right on the Equator. My last day in the southern hemisphere. I'd decided to cross the line at 23° west, in search of northerly winds. Around here there is a kind of void between the two Atlantic winds; a place of flat calms and sudden storms. The south-east trade winds, which had brought me up from South Africa in a safe, straight corridor of wind, would cease just after the Equator, and until I picked up the corresponding trade winds on the northern side, the north-easterlies, I'd have to sail through this strip of meteorological indecision known as the doldrums.

Incredible traffic. Squadrons of flying fish taking off one after the other, always against the wind, as they described long arcs over the waves: from *Paratii*'s deck I watched thousands of these small flying creatures, gliding through the air in successive waves.

During May the doldrums, this zone of equatorial convergence, spread further southward, from around latitude 5° north to the Equator. I'd organised a little celebration for the moment when I actually crossed the Equator: 'So long, Southern Hemisphere. Here we go to the land of the midnight sun!' It is not simply the crossing

of an imaginary line: a threatening sky, heavy clouds, rain
and thunder, with sudden shafts of very strong sunshine
falling on an oily sea – you have a real impression of a
physical frontier between two oceans and their systems.
And suffocating heat. During thunderstorms I had all the
freshwater showers one could ask for; naked on deck, a
piece of soap in my hand, the towel hanging on the sheets,
sometimes waiting for the next burst of rain to wash the
soap off. Seeing the clean and fresh water pouring down
the boom like a waterfall, I invented a water collector at
the bottom of the sail. This was soon transformed into a
hanging swimming pool. The actual crossing took a little
more than a day, and then with a small push from the
engine. But at 3° north, I met steady winds again. Behind
were more than three weeks of beautiful, sunny sailing
days, following the very special landfall.

A high-speed life, smiling, on my bike, flying around
the streets of Cape Town, swapping stories with people
on boats from all over the world, distant friends who
couldn't tear themselves away. The affection of Nina
– my adoptive mother – who couldn't come on board
because of her bad spine, but who left fresh fruit on the
deck each morning. An important stop because I also
saw Adrian Artman, a Cape coloured who seven years
before had given me his only navigation compass. I had
used it on all my journeys since then, working out and
measuring distances on all sorts of charts. He was my
official supplier of maps and navigation literature. In two
weeks Adrian telephoned all over the world to muster an
arsenal of documents I urgently needed and that I couldn't
find anywhere. These charts were one of the reasons for
my stop in Cape Town. He also obtained for me the maps
of the Norwegian and the Spitsbergen Seas that were now
lying on my chart table. Leaving Cape Town, I didn't yet
know what was to be my next stop. I had thought about
some still undefined point between the Shetlands, Norway

and Iceland before finally reaching the ice. Nevertheless, I knew precisely where I wanted to get to.

If I were to reach the Arctic at the start of the season as planned, I had to make up time. So I decided that if all went well I wouldn't stop anywhere before reaching latitude 60° north. This meant that a number of interesting ports I had been dreaming about – Lüderitz (a kind of Paraty set beside the Namibian desert), St Helena and Ascension Island – would all have to wait for another journey.

It was Pancho, a Brazilian whom I'd met on my first day in Cape Town, who loosed the ropes on the sad day of departure. He turned out to be a neighbour in the same street back in São Paulo and also in Paraty, somebody whom strangely, I'd never met before. Pancho had just crossed the Atlantic on board a yacht, the *Tao*, and was now planning to sail to Spain in a month's time. But the person who finally went in his place was Esmeralda, a crazy Englishwoman whom we met at the Royal Cape Yacht Club, the human zoo where I had been anchored.

Oddly enough, later I heard on the Durban maritime radio network that they'd just found a woman called Esmeralda. She had been shipwrecked on a yacht that had run aground on the Skeleton Coast near Lüderitz. The very same person. So Pancho, the most famous juggler in the Yacht Club circus, had escaped a good adventure.

Now I was right in the middle of the trade winds, regular seas and good weather. *Paratii* was cutting through wind and wave as she made her way northwards. Under full sail, the boat heeled over to starboard, I realised that sailing into the wind is not necessarily as hellish as it might seem. The alarm clock carried on its infernal round of going off every forty-five minutes, but I did have short periods of good sleep. Otherwise I spent most of my time in the companionway on the windward side – to which I transferred the meal service, as it was the highest spot.

Eating Chinese sweet-and-sour chicken with chopsticks,

plate on my lap, feet over the side, I noticed something strange on deck. I ran my finger over the bright paint: it was coated with a reddish dust. I couldn't believe it. Looking upwards, I could no longer see anything white. On the windward side the sails, radio antenna, deck – everything was coloured red. Nine hundred miles from the Senegal coast, right in the middle of the Atlantic, the boat was covered in fine Saharan dust. The desert was crossing the ocean. How many things happen on a non-stop journey. There had only been sea since I left, and there would only be sea until I arrived. Yet so much was happening around me: so many new and different seascapes, despite being composed of the same elements.

New, bigger birds, now solitary. A whole fleet of Portuguese men-of-war, small blue jellyfish sailing in the same direction, a child's plastic potty, pieces of a container and even an entire Russian ship: the list of passing objects and beings was endless.

Five hundred miles west of the Cape Verde Islands, having decided, in order to fix the position for the day, I had to point the sextant to the south, no longer to the north. I had crossed the point of latitude at which the sun declined that day – 20°. The landscape of the night sky was completely new, dominated by Ursa Major, with the incredible Pole Star right in the centre. 'How simple finding true north is in a place like this,' I thought, looking at the small polar star. The whole night sky, at an elevation roughly equal to one's own latitude, revolves around this point. The further I went north, the higher it would stand in the sky, exactly in the direction I was going.

It was easy to understand why in the past it was so much safer to navigate in the northern hemisphere. Unfortunately in the southern hemisphere there isn't any comparable star at the polar zenith that can be used as a permanent guide to direction and reference for determining latitude. I pointed the prow to true north until I reached the latitude of the Azores. *Paratii* had sailed for sixteen days on the same tack and I had got so used to sloping to the left, that on the first day I went about, I had an internal cataclysm.

Supporting myself against the walls, I got used to walking on the left. Rubbish and bits and pieces had begun to accumulate on one side. When I tacked, everything swung to the right, the silver bookmark Armelle had made me, the dividers, tapes, tools, books, dishes and all sorts of instruments came out of their corners and flew across the boat. Taking care of the sails, I could only listen to the cacophony.

From the Azores onwards, I began a course correction toward the north-east, having decided to stop at a place I'd heard very little about – Thorshavn – the capital of the Faeroe Islands, which was now less than 2,000 miles north.

Leaving the 'marine motorway' that the trade winds form, work with the sails increased, and during tacking manoeuvres or when bringing down sail I had to watch out for the 'vipers' that lay restless and deep in the cockpit.

Until I crossed the North Atlantic's high-pressure centre and found the westerly winds getting firmer, there were variable wind directions, and from time to time a strong blow. During the fifteenth century the understanding of the mechanisms that determine atmospheric pressure and the winds was probably the most critical obstacle to west-bound navigation. The real achievement of Christopher Colombus's first expedition of 1492 was surmounting this obstacle. By studying modern marine charts and pilot's instructions for the North Atlantic – which these days are compiled with the aid of computers and satellites – it's obvious that Columbus's landfall in America is a minor achievement compared with the importance of his real discovery – the route and the return. Intuitively perhaps, the Genoan found the ideal route, at this time the only one, to reach the Antilles and to return to the Iberian Peninsula. The anticyclonic turn around the Azores.

An incredibly easy navigation route, nothing like the challenges in getting round the tip of Africa in order to set course for India, or even sailing in the Mediterranean. But a route that could be found only by a person who was brave enough to do it.

Other contemporary and perceived obstacles to navigation – perhaps even graver ones – weren't even real, such as the well-known Cape Bojador, in the western Sahara. The Portuguese poet Fernando Pessoa wrote:

> *Quem quer passar além do Bojador*
> *Tem que passar além da dor.*
>
> *If you want to go beyond the Bojador*
> *You have to go beyond pain.*

From 1424 to 1434, fifteen expeditions tried to pass this much-feared cape. All of them failed and returned. It became an imaginary barrier that in fact is no more than a tiny promontory with some hidden shoals: a symbol of fear, of lack of courage at a time when navigation meant only following the coast. Gil Eanes, who first crossed it in 1434, after a previously unsuccessful attempt, described it as 'effectively uncrossable'. 'The currents are so strong that a boat which crosses them would never be able to come back ...' claims Zurara's *Crónica dos Feitos da Guiné* (Chronicle of Guinea Expeditions). It was the symbol of one prince's courage – Henry the Navigator – who, not believing in 'uncrossable capes', demolished fear and insisted until they succeeded. The fact is there are many Bojadors at sea, most of the obstacles to great voyages are smaller than their size.

The west wind finally came from America over the Azores, while I was reading all about it.

The wind you don't respect is always an obstacle. I remembered the seventy-knot gale in the Drake Passage that took me with such speed out of Antarctica. And the pieces of iceberg fast inside Marguerite Bay, which for two days protected *Paratii* from bad weather. They too were like Cape Bojador, until the moment I entered them. We face other Bojadors when we build a boat, the cold, for example, 'it will destroy your boat, freeze your life,' many people said. And then, discovering that the cold, rather than being an obstacle, was an ally, a synonym for comfort, well-being, safety. Dry, cold, sunny Antarctic days collecting mussels, shirtless on Casabianca Island.

Now it was cold, but an irritating humid cold of 15°C. Thinking about currents and ready to enter the arm that veers northwards from the Gulf Stream, I remembered the Nescafé jar which had just been finished. An idea, why not, talking of currents? I put a valueless 100,000-cruzeiro Brazilian banknote – one of those stamped all over with zeroes – into the jar. In went a shocking-pink sailor's knot tied around one of the penguin-pebbles and a radio ham's message form with my address, asking the person who found the bottle please to send it to me in Brazil. I noted down my position and the date: 'Lat. 49°49'N, Long. 23°49'W, 4 June 1991, S/Y *Paratii*, sailing from Cape Town to Faeroe Islands.' I closed it tightly and threw it on the water.

The ideal would have been a plastic bottle which wouldn't break if thrown against the rocks. A dozen bottles would have been even better. But anyway I knew that the chances of drifting bottles being picked up was around 5 per cent and I wasn't at all keen on the idea of emptying out twenty bottles of anything on board. This was the only bottle I threw overboard during the whole journey, and I never imagined that seven months later I would receive a letter with a picture of a ten-year-old Norwegian boy, happily holding the little shocking-pink ball with its small Antarctic stone and a strange banknote he'd found.

At the back of the pilot chart I was using for the month of June was an interesting story about drift in the North Atlantic. On March 1888 the three-masted American schooner W. L. *White* had been abandoned in Delaware Bay, near New York. She was taking on water and there was no one aboard. After ten months adrift, her position plotted by forty-five other ships, and crossing 5,000 miles of Atlantic, she finally went aground, ramshackle, in the north of Scotland. But she didn't sink.

Some ships – and ideas – can be so strong they don't need a crew to cross an ocean. *Paratii*, although not drifting, had sailed 17,000 miles since leaving Brazil, and I had not spent more than seven hours on the tiller. The rest of the time either Florence or the automatic pilot was in control. Neither presented problems that I couldn't resolve.

For three days I dreamed of the drifting of W. L. *White*, which must have found different winds in this region. There was a strong depression between my current position and the Hebrides, with head-winds of 35 to 45 knots and confused seas. Zigzagging against the weather, I had to pass north of Rockall, that lonely rock in the ocean, before the Atlantic finally calmed down.

There were still two days to go before arriving at the Faeroes. I hadn't the slightest idea what the islands would look like. I would have to be very careful with tides running between them. There were currents of up to twelve knots, changing every hour. A group of huge dolphins appeared on the bow. They didn't move when I approached, and I noticed they were in fact whales, small black pilot whales. On all sides, hundreds of whales, a sign of my arrival in a new country. In mysteriously calm, cloudy weather, I completed a 58-day ocean crossing, having been out of sight of land since Cape Town; sleeping heavily, for the first time I missed one of my 45-minute wake-up calls. I awoke to see a light rain on the windows and hear a curious noise.

One o'clock in the morning. The sun was just starting to rise, and someone was calling on channel 16 in a completely incomprehensible language. There beside *Paratii* was a Nordic fishing boat. Right in front was Sydero Island. Thanks for the warning.

At 8:50, after going past impressive cliffs and crossing through narrow, deep channels, I finally reached the harbour of Thorshavn with the radar going at full blast to get me through a fog as thick as pea-soup.

A veritable Toytown appeared out of the mist, with ancient and colourful houses built on the rocks. Some roofs were covered with green grass, where the wind made waves as on fields of wheat. When *Paratii's* hull touched the fenders on the quay I felt like letting out a scream, a scream of happiness. Instead, a pleasant gentleman appeared out of the rain, soaking wet, to catch the painter and help me tie *Paratii* up. I moored in the centre of the town. Stepping on to the concrete quay, I felt as if I was stepping into a dream.

On a small stone peninsula in the middle of the port, just ninety metres from where I was moored, the local parliament had been established in AD 825 by Vikings coming from Norway. Called the Logting, it is the oldest functioning parliament in the world. The archipelago rising in the fog, was out of a fairy tale. I had never imagined anything like it.

Before taking my bicycle out of the boat, I had already completed all the immigration formalities. It only took around ninety seconds, and the police officers helped me by taking away two months of rubbish bags. I received four invitations to visit different houses in the town, another invitation to play on the town football ground, covered with artificial grass, and yet another to swim in the municipal heated swimming pool. I didn't think twice before accepting this last invitation.

The Faeroe islanders are descendants of the Vikings who left for Iceland between the eighth and ninth centuries AD, and have a humour and good nature rare among other Scandinavians. There are only 47,000 of them, scattered across eighteen islands and seventy small towns set on the cliffs, and their land now forms part of Denmark. The twenty-five largest towns have ports for big ships and everyone lives off the sea. It's either fishing, salmon-farming or building ships. By working on and in the sea, they have managed to create one of the highest living standards in the world. They also have the world's most modern fishing fleet.

Simple, straightforward and hardworking people, they are very proud of their small, rich islands and take pleasure in those rare visitors who go there. During my visit, there was going to be an invasion of tourists on the island: a total of three. After a year and a half, I was going to see my sister Cabeluda, and Alvaro and Cris. They were coming for a week's visit to *Paratii*, a real migration into the Viking domain.

During these weeks I gathered vital information for anyone who lives on boats. I got to know skippers and fishermen who were used to fishing in waters all over the world, but especially in the Arctic. So I filled my boat up with stories, with books and with plans for building Viking boats.

Invited to visit a salmon farm, I realised why this small nation is so rich, and, after work, so happy. I nearly lost my fingers through cold and tiredness, pulling live salmon from the tanks. Blue-eyed girls operating the machines or driving the tractors. The men, many of advanced age, spending more than twelve hours in the water on the floating fish cages. Young and old working hard together. There were no employees, all were partners in this shared asset: the sea.

I kept up with the progress of the pack ice around Greenland, Iceland and Spitsbergen as I hitched rides on their fishing boats – for most of them were equipped with fantastic electronic weather stations and fishing laboratories (where studies on reproductive habits and density of fish species were carried out).

It was still early, and there was far too much ice in the north. So I spent a welcome stay of eighteen days in this Viking country, almost turning pink from all the salmon I received from nameless fishermen, who would leave them on the deck in the early morning.

Before leaving with Cabeluda, Cris bought and sent home, via *Paratii*, one of those heaters that all the Faeroe boats have. It was to be installed in her own boat, the brave little *Plâncton*, back in Porto Alegre in Brazil. Even during the warm summer in the Faeroes, I would keep my heater on all the time to make sure the boat was dry and comfortable. The kettle was always on the hotplate, making coffee for visitors took a few seconds.

On the last day of June, *Paratii* said goodbye to all the boats and friends we had met, and left a berth in a harbour where it would be easy to grow moss on the mooring ropes. At half-past nine I stowed my bicycle, and made ready the sails, while the engine soon took us out to the open sea. Gradually, those gigantic thousand-metre-high cliffs were lost in the distance.

I opened the British nautical chart No. 4010 – the one to reach Spitsbergen – and the log. Distracted, I began to scribble calculations.

Suddenly a strange engine noise. I put my head out, surprised, as I was already far from the islands. Maybe it was a Viking pirate assault: two fellows travelling at high speed in a tiny rubber boat, both completely drunk, slowed down beside me. Trying to stand up while holding on to his bottle, one of them shouted:

'Hey, you, Brazilian, do you want a beer?'

'No, thank you, thank you', I answered, without thinking too much.

'I don't know what you are searching for up there, but
have a wonderful trip!' And they went off, in zigzags,
back to the islands. I should have accepted that beer.
Great people, the Faeroe islanders.

14

GATHERING THE PEBBLES

S ixteen thousand nautical miles and the entire Atlantic Ocean from one end to the other, since the last encounter with ice. *Paratii* was now completely surrounded by small pieces of brash ice covering the surface of water so still that it resembled a mirror, on whose flat surface I saw an upside-down boat, identical to mine. A real mirror, with ice arranged around the border like embroidery, reflecting the mountains around Kongsfjord and the beautiful peninsula of Blomstrandhalvoya. A week before, I had arrived in Spitsbergen – the largest island in the Svalbard group – after a peaceful and uneventful journey. The approach lay through Longyearbyen on Isfjorden, not a very interesting place, but I managed to get navigation data there, including Norwegian navigation map No. 521, the only one missing from my collection, which would allow me to reach Moffen Island.

The brash ice that glinted around me was the remains of an interesting phenomenon which had just taken place. The huge glacier that came from Haakon VII Land had collapsed in pieces, opening a channel in the peninsula so that the point where I was anchored had now became an island. What a spectacle! I don't know why, but I thought that *Paratii* could pass through this channel and come out on the other side, and so inaugurate a channel that hadn't existed previously and was not marked on any map. Just the kind of bad idea one can have when hypnotised by the beauty of a place.

For the first time, *Paratii* ran badly aground. It was a terrible spot. There were great walls of ice on both sides, which kept on releasing slices bigger than a house; there were also sharp pointed rocks and thick mud which fastened itself to the bottom of the keel. As the tide was high I had made a serious mistake and I had to find a way out of this trap quickly, forcing a passage with the help of the motor, hitting invisible rocks. The blows were so strong that even the famous blue carry-all was spilt, scattering over the workshop those gentoo pebbles I had carried so far. Anxious minutes until I found the way out of this maze of submerged dangers and brought *Paratii* back into deep waters. Safe at last, I put the pebbles back in the blue bag and *Paratii* left the underwater rocks in peace.

On the other side of the bay I visited Ny Alesund, a small miners' village, where the Norskpolarinstitut is situated. A little beyond the buildings is a monument in a field, where I sat down. In May 1926 Roald Amundsen left this spot, together with Lincoln Ellsworth and Umberto Nobile, to start his historic crossing of the northern polar ice-cap in a Zeppelin, the *Norge*, which landed two days later in Teller on the Alaskan side after flying over the North Pole. Just before the *Norge* took off, Commander Richard E. Byrd and Floyd Bennet had turned up with an aeroplane in which they planned to complete the first return flight over the pole. Instead of arguments over who should go down in the history books for this 'first', there were gentlemanly manners. Amundsen insisted that Byrd should go first and waited until his return. Only after the pole had been reached did Amundsen leave in the *Norge*. The success of the first air crossing of the Arctic resulted in a tragic accident. Amundsen and Nobile quarrelled after the flight and two years later, in 1928, Nobile set out in another Zeppelin, the *Italia*, to repeat the crossing without Amundsen. The *Italia* suffered an accident and temporarily disappeared. While a rescue was being organised, Amundsen – either in a gesture of reconciliation or simply as a challenge – left to rescue Nobile in a French Latham 47 aeroplane. Nobile was eventually rescued by another expedition, but the Latham 47 was never seen again.

During that first week in Spitsbergen, I met three big boats that had attempted to travel northwards from the island but had given up after finding too much ice. 'Brazilian, you won't ever get through,' they warned. 'This year you won't do it.' 'Well,' I thought, 'we shall see.' If it wasn't possible to reach little Moffen Island, it wouldn't be the end of me. The truth is that not all ice is 'impassable', and the only way of finding out was to try. At this stage in such a long journey, the failure would be not to try.

That same week I met another boat which had just arrived from Norway. The *Sam* was a beautiful French yacht, also built from aluminium, though with much finer plates. Aboard were three men and a woman, all from Brittany. We decided to try crossing north in two boats.

On the the morning of 20 June *Paratii* finally got into the pack ice, a formidable expanse of floating ice, stretching endlessly from Greenland to the Bering Strait, and from Siberia to Alaska, an entire frozen sea. A strange sensation of conditional freedom, with channels or leads opening and closing amongst huge ice plates that could delay a boat for hours, or even until the following summer. Yet there was always a new way opening, so I continued northward as far as I could, sometimes breaking the sharp points of ice that I couldn't avoid. When missing the leads, the bows would sometimes climb a little over the ice before sliding back. With a much less robust hull, *Sam* followed behind at a distance. Tense sailing, full of surprises.

Decision-taking caused permanent stress. 'Which way should I go?' In front were dozens and dozens of dead-end leads with no way through, or very narrow channels where we had to wait for the ice to open further. Moffen was to the east, but the only passage was to the north. Visibility had fallen down to a few metres, and then, it was no longer possible to choose unobstructed channels. I began to leave red paint-marks on every iceberg we touched.

At 20:39 GMT, the GPS showed latitude 80° north, and longitude 11° 28′ 47 east. At midnight I halted. There was nowhere further for *Paratii* to go. I couldn't see the *Sam* through the fog, but I knew from the radar she was almost a mile away from me.

I climbed up the mast for the twentieth time. Nowhere to get through. More than twenty hours without sleep, constantly struggling to find the right direction. I couldn't stop now, so close to the end. Rolph and Deborah of the *Northern Light*, whom I had met the previous summer before leaving Antarctica, had been here and had been forced to give up some few miles from Moffen, with a huge feeling of frustration.

I ran inside to get some sweets or dried fruits from the kitchen, planning to eat them on deck. In a place like that you might stay for a few hours or several months, you never know. I returned, feeling optimistic and carrying a package of 'one day's emergency ration' while chewing a chocolate bar. I saw a ball in the sky. 'I can't believe it!' The sun, little by little, growing more visible, the fog becoming more transparent as it steadily lifted. I climbed up the mast once again with my binoculars. Then I saw a fairly wide channel to the north. I had to turn about quickly and find a way out to the north. In the distance a group of walruses, the first I had seen, were resting beside the channel.

With less than fifteen miles to go, it was difficult to know just how far I could go on. At 3:10 GMT, 5:10 local time, I knew I was really close. But I could see nothing more than an ocean covered by ice blocks, and to the south Spitsbergen Island and Haakon VII Land. Once again, I climbed up the mast to the first spreader, then to the second. Then, among those huge ice blocks I saw a blank space. Looking through my binoculars, which I carried around my neck, there it was: Moffen Island. This dream, which had seemed so distant, was now very close.

It was 3:40 GMT when I dropped the anchor into three-metre-deep water. Fifteen minutes later the *Sam* anchored a little further to the north. What a joy! What ferocious joy!

I turned *Vagabundo* the right side up, set it on the water and, rowing with the last oar from Paraty that had survived, I found a block of ice that had run aground. This was where I threw my other anchor. Moffen Island is no more than a narrow ring of small stones two metres high; the island is a triangular pear-shape with a lagoon at its centre. Two miles long, it is the only place reserved for breeding walruses in Spitsbergen. I found all sorts of wrack there: driftwood that had come from Siberia, plastics from all over the world, nylon rope, fishing-net floats. Between *Paratii* and the island large pieces of ice were floating in, and behind them I could see one of those famous fog banks coming up. Staying there any longer was risky. The channels were changing their position and if the fog caught us it would be difficult to get back.

The Moffen Island interlude didn't last for more than three hours. To get there it had taken me five months sailing from latitude 68° south to 80° north, thousands of miles in order to spend just three hours there. Three eternal and wonderful hours. Before getting back on board, I gathered some small pebbles I found on the way, all the same shape as the island, and at 8:40 I raised anchor to start my return. It was then that *Paratii* turned her prow southward. Towards home.

Not because the island was so far from home, so high in latitude, so difficult to get to, but because for so long it was the place I had dreamed of reaching, Moffen had become the summit of a long and beautiful escalator.

All that was left was a blue bag full of pebbles. The most precious stones that anyone could possess.

* * *

Pebbles from both the north and the south were mixed together in the blue bag. Now the only thing that would bring me peace was to return home. It wasn't easy to get out of the pack ice, but by the end of that day – 21 July – we were again sailing in free waters. *Sam* was to sail back to Kongsfjord and I decided to go straight back to Brazil. I had a long way to go before reaching Jurumirim, and this was the only place I wanted to be.

I don't like farewells. Yet parting from *Sam* was wonderful because we never said goodbye. We were sailing, side by side, in front of the paradisiacal entrance to Magdalenafjord, the sun shining strongly, the sea peaceful. They knew I wasn't going to sail into the fjord. They were all sitting on the side of the boat with no one on the rudder, all facing the same direction, watching *Paratii* and smiling. A few hours before they had given me a couple of fresh loaves, a *pâté maison* and tin of *rillettes de canard*, from Fauchon, at '26 Place de la Madeleine, Paris'. 'You won't have time to cook when you're on the high seas. Have a safe trip back to Brazil.' I could have yelled out something, we were still within earshot. I too was sitting over the gunwales, smiling, silently looking across at them.

A thick bank of fog was right in front and, before we realised, it was too late even for a farewell gesture. We were all engulfed by the fog, smiling, each proceeding in his own direction.

*   *   *

A profound sense of well-being and calm took over on board. What before had frightened or caused worry, now only set me thinking. Through these windows – where I could see only fog or wind-filled sails – I had seen all the images that I wished to see. And I had touched them. There is no purer or truer way to experience places than to touch them with the keel of a boat. Or with your own fingers. The simplest and most universal way of caring. The touch.

I could sail *Paratii* with my fingertips, for now I felt the boat in an entirely different way. In the beginning any noises, banging, groans, or the whistling of the wind would cause me anxiety. Making mistakes and learning from them, crashing against the ice, into waves and even into rocks, I discovered the origins of sounds and the limits of my red sailing machine. Earlier, if I was caught by a wave while up in the bows and received a drenching, even in the tropics, I'd scream and protest against the elements. Now, despite the cold and the snow, an unexpected soaking would produce no more reaction from me than to wipe the dripping hair from my eyes with the back of my hand, and continue whistling. Perhaps a certain hardening, an indifference to pain and discomfort that the sea instils had taken over, as fishermen from the north say. I don't know, perhaps it is more than that. A greater sense of what is really important.

I was making a sandwich in the galley with the homemade bread, when I felt, down in my guts, a violent blow. I stopped chewing. 'What now?' There was silence. 'If I'd collided with a Russian ship we'd know about it by now.' I went up on deck, sandwich in hand. Perhaps it had been ice, but I couldn't see any, just see a few lines in the water ahead. Before I could guess what they were, I felt a series of heavy, booming blows. Logs in the water. Tree trunks! I had twice crashed into driftwood, logs that had floated down from the Siberian rivers, and then got stuck in the Arctic pack ice, drifting perhaps for centuries before being spat out close to the Greenland coast. In Spitsbergen I had been very impressed by the volume of driftwood; thousands of tree trunks piled up in bays and slopes facing the open sea. In a land where there isn't a single tree it is always possible to make a fire, using these scraps of wood, virtually anywhere. In Iceland, too, the collection of driftwood has always been an important part of the northern village life.

Not only trees but many kinds of floating detritus travel through the pack ice to end up in places very distant from their places of origin. One of these was a piece of the *Jeanette*, an American ship which in 1881 had been wrecked in the ice near Severnaya Zemlia in northern Siberia. Many years later wreckage from the *Jeanette* was found on the south coast of Greenland, and so became the first concrete evidence to support the theory of transpolar drift. This was to inspire Fridtjof Nansen in his attempt to reach the North Pole with *Fram*, drifting in the ice from Siberia for three years.

There hadn't been any damage from the logs, but if *Paratii* had been built of fibreglass or of concrete I would have had an interesting excuse for my shipwreck: 'I crashed into some Siberian trees, close to Iceland.'

Return. Going home was all that I now wished for, and I found out just how difficult it is to interrupt one's return journey, even if only for a rest. Nothing in the world could make me rest before I touched Brazil again.

The only stop during the journey down from Moffen Island was on Iceland's east coast. I had to wait in Seydisfjordur for a spare wind-vane rudder I had ordered from Sweden, which I might use on some future expedition. On this stop I suffered a mishap that I had managed to avoid during my entire two years of travel.

I plunged into a fog bank and, being without any detailed

chart of Iceland's coast, I was forced to make a completely blind approach. I turned on the depth sounder and the radar scanner about ten miles from the coast because the wind was so strong. Still no sight of land. Five miles from the coast and I hadn't seen a thing. I considered the possibility of waiting out at sea in deep water until the fog lifted, but that might have turned out to be even more dangerous. By two o'clock it still had not begun to grow light and I was only 1,000 metres away from the coast, tacking up and down. Eyes glued to the radar monitor, whose image magnification was now switched to the maximum, I still couldn't see any sign of Iceland. It's not possible! A few seconds more and I would be breaking my nose on the cliffs. The entrance to the deep fjord couldn't be more that a few hundred metres away. Impossible! I loosened the sheets and dropped the mainsail, I wasn't prepared to wreck my boat on the island where Charcot had sunk together with his beloved *Pourquoi pas?*. There were puffins all around on the sea, and the cliffs should have been only a few metres in front. Then a great moon rose from out of the fog and two huge cliffs appeared, with a channel between them. The entrance to Seydisfjordur. Once inside the fjord there was neither fog nor the slightest wind. I turned on the engine, amazed at the spectacle of those high escarpments and waterfalls reflected in the channel's quiet waters, as though in a mirror. Twelve miles further inside this magical place I saw the lights of a small town reflected on the water. I had no idea where to moor, and went past the quay twice, searching for a place while I looked upward at the silvery mountains. At last I tied up at a twisted and abandoned wooden jetty. I jumped off, mooring rope in my hand, and gently tied up *Paratii*. With the engine off, the silence was astonishing; the moon still shone brightly even though the day was dawning. I have never stopped in such a beautiful place, never come so near to bursting. As I wasn't sleepy I assembled my

187

bicycle, tidied things up a bit inside the boat and set off, pedalling through the sleeping town. An enchanted place. Nobody on the streets. I rode until I saw a petrol station with its lights on, its doors open, yet deserted. I returned to the boat, found everything was fine, so I slept a bit.

In the morning I spent just five minutes completing immigration formalities. I went to a coffee shop, beautiful but empty. Nobody to speak to. Not quite so beautiful. Back to the boat with nothing to do, everything perfectly shipshape. I almost left without waiting for the wind vane. Waiting five days was difficult. With relief I took a final glance at this silent volcanic land as the high glacial peaks of Vatnajökull disappeared below the horizon.

Paratii was relieved of unnecessary anchors, chains and other irons, as well as lubricating oils I would no longer need. An emergency inflatable dinghy was folded on the deck, and everything that could be swept away by the wind was carefully tied down. September is not the best month for a non-stop journey south. Winds and currents are against you and bad weather is frequent.

Travelling south from the Arctic Circle, temperatures were not so low, but life was a lot less comfortable due to the humidity, strong winds and unsettled seas to the south of Iceland. Or, maybe on second thoughts, it was not so bad. Lying back, feeling the boat slicing through the waves, I imagined how, ten centuries before, boats had made crossings identical to this, sailing between the islands of Europe, the south of Iceland, Greenland and America. Fantastic boats they used, which still have much to teach about design and technology. When, in the ninth and tenth centuries, the Vikings arrived in Iceland from Norway, they brought with them much more than cattle, Celtic slaves, tools and weapons. Their boats were scarcely bigger than *Paratii*, carrying fifteen to twenty men each, yet from the year 1,000 they transported an entire culture condensed into book form – the Viking Sagas. And this at a time when books scarcely existed in Europe. The *Landnämabók* is a manual of nautical instructions with instructions on how to undertake the crossings between the Shetland Islands, Faeroe Islands, Iceland and Greenland. The northern peoples, in their wanderings through the eleventh century, didn't set out to discover America, but to colonise it. In Vinland or Newfoundland, Gudrid Thorbjarnardóttir gave birth to Snorre, the only white boy to be born in the Americas prior to the arrival of the Spanish, 500 years later. She was a Viking woman travelling with Eric the Red during the colonisation of Greenland. She married first Leif Eriksson's brother, who was killed in America, and then later Thorfinn. It was a colonisation which didn't last for more than three years, because after that, they were expelled by the *Skrälingar*, as they called the American Indians.

The Viking longships or *knorr* were superb boats and their sailors even more extraordinary. They criss-crossed this part of the Atlantic with a network of navigation routes that no other nation has since been able to repeat. To understand what Eric's descendants achieved and to understand what sailing in the North Atlantic involves, one needs both to have seen a replica of a longship on the water and to have sailed a modern fifteen-metre sailing yacht.

On the night of 20 August, I was sailing through the 'accursed region' of the North Atlantic in the area between Ireland and Greenland. The weather was nightmarish and I made a bad mistake when putting the boat about. The jib split and flew into tatters. It could have been worse, it might have taken the mast as well. I put up the spare sail and in a couple of days had avoided the danger of having to make a landfall in Ireland. Now the winds were in my favour and even if I'd only had a simple squaresail – like a longship – I would still have been able to reach the Equator quickly, and soon after that, Jurumirim.

I became a nightly listener to a formidable radio ham, a lady from Curitiba, Brazil, called America, PY 5 AEV. I used her to send messages and she was able to give me the news from Brazil. News! How I missed a newspaper with my breakfast. Just something to read. Lately I had been reading the *Svalbard Treatise*, which I had bought in Ny Alesund, and then a book given to me by Professor Villela that I had almost lost.

Early one morning I was having breakfast on the 'verandah' when I heard two explosions, one after the other, like shots. Though the sea was calm I was so surprised that my breakfast ended up on the deck and Villela's book – *The Roots of Coincidence* by Arthur Koestler – almost landed up in the Atlantic. Above me two supersonic aeroplanes had just gone through the sound barrier.

The first of September. The first flying fishes. Back to the trade winds! What an ocean of happiness a small flying fish can bring one. At last I had reached the watery highway that runs down the Atlantic as far as the Equator. In the night sky the Pole Star was now thirty degrees high, the same elevation as my own latitude.

Florence had undergone a complete overhaul. I replaced the control cables and put grease on all the axles. One thousand eight hundred nautical miles to this line that separates the hemispheres. The distance was still great, but at least I was certain that I would meet no more bad weather.

On a fabulously sunny day I went back to reading Koestler's book. Our position was about 600 miles north of the Equator and I sat at the foot of the mast just like a naked Hindu with my legs crossed, the little book in my lap. Then I heard a funny sound, like a sail flapping. The sea was calm, the wind following, all the sails were filled and visibility was perfect. We were also well away from the main navigation routes. Every forty-five minutes, the alarm clock faithfully sounded its warning, and I scarcely took my eyes from the page. The flapping noise continued but I didn't get up to trim the sails, because the wind was manageable. That sail could wait a bit. Suddenly the noise increased. When I lifted my eyes I was completely paralysed. Through the genoa a grey steel wall with the name *Mar Frio* written in gigantic letters, was sliding by. An Argentine ship full speed on a collision course. There were less than 100 metres between us and I was going to hit the ship right in the middle. There were lots of Argentinians on deck. In a panic I jumped up and the first idea that occurred me was to look for my pair of shorts. There was no time for such madness, as sailing boats have no brakes. I disconnected the automatic pilot and, using brute force, tried to turn the rudder. Not one of the easiest things when a boat is under full sail. I missed the ship by a fraction, sliding under the stern of the *Mar Frio*, cutting right through her wake. Because of the tack I was on, it wasn't clear whether the ship ought really to have given way to me. But in cases like this, being in the right isn't the point. The best thing is to give other boats a wide berth. I couldn't sleep properly for two days afterwards. It's easy to make unpardonable mistakes even in calm waters with a following wind.

Now the Pole Star had disappeared below the horizon and I crossed into the southern hemisphere under a battering of thunderstorms and heavy rain. At 12:48 GMT, on 23 September – the equinox – I noted on my log: 'Welcome, Spring.' Soon afterwards, I stole a line from Fernando Pessoa:

> Oh salty sea, how much of your salt
> are tears from Portugal . . .

Paratii looked like a salt-works, covered with Portugal's tears. Occasional bursts of spray soaked the deck and then dried out in the strong sun, leaving a thin layer of salt, as white as snow.

With each day we drew nearer. One thousand four hundred and sixty-eight miles to Joatinga! On 29 September I moved into the area covered by Brazilian navigation chart No. 70 – from Belmonte to Rio de Janeiro. These waters were well known to me and my feelings were strong. Then a swift, looking very wet and bedraggled, established residence on the steering platform. Whenever I approached, it would fly up on to the radar antenna without bothering to get any further away. It was good to have company now.

On the weekly broadcast with Alvaro I learned that Hermann had already left the Hanseática shipyard near São Paulo aboard *Rapa Nui*, heading for Paraty. But when? On 3 October, after a fine demonstration of how strong and unsettled the sea could be in 'warning area B' adjacent to the offshore oil platforms of the Campos basin, a small school of humpback whales passed close by me. The water-logged swift flew away and the wind dropped. But the short choppy sea made progress slow.

It was a dark night and the sky overcast. Later on, a very weak halo of light broke free of the clouds to the north. My God! The lights of Rio de Janeiro, shining beyond the horizon.

At 9:00 GMT, I had radio contact with Alvaro. There were no difficulties with the transmission, but his voice sounded nervous. He asked for my position and if I could give him an estimate of my arrival time. 'I don't have the position, Alvaro. I'm fifteen miles south-east of Joatinga. Brazil is dead ahead and it looks beautiful!' Like a distant dream, the land was tinged with blue and only little by little gained contour and detail, slowly turning green.

At 14:10 I crossed in front of Joatinga, in the direction of Ponta Grossa in Paraty. All around were the islands I knew so well. A small dark spot was approaching. A sailing boat. I grabbed the binoculars and made out two masts, a blue hull. *Rapa Nui* was approaching under motor, her sails down, as there was no wind. A thick haze infused the surrounding mountains and islands with a vivid and intense green the like of which I had never seen. Still holding my binoculars, I propped myself on the mast to see who was on board. I could make out the golden, shiny hair of Cabeluda, and also Hermann with his red coat, and two other friends.

Next to Coconut Palm Island I once again heard the familiar siren of *Rapa Nui*. Then they turned and approached. Cabeluda was by the tiller, with both arms raised, something in her hands. It was a tin of beer and an orange, which I caught in the air. The two best presents I ever had. I kept the tin and with my faithful black penknife I cut the orange from one pole to the other, in four pieces.

We sailed side by side, the four of them on board the blue schooner laughing. Sailing together once again. *Paratii* still had a blue scratch-mark from *Rapa Nui*, which she had got on her maiden voyage near Joatinga when both boats had been too close together. Passing Ponta Grossa, I could see the pale contours of the town, its white houses contrasting with the dark hills behind. There was the church and the imperial palm trees. Over there on the left was our corner, Jurumirim Bay.

It was about three o'clock in the afternoon, but I can't remember the exact time. I entered the small hidden bay in silence. Close to the beach I dropped anchor while the boat was still moving. The chain rattled out, straightened and *Paratii*'s bow swung quietly around. The anchor held, the sails were stowed, the motor turned off. Silence. Phew!

So I was back again, to *exactly* the same strip of sand I had left twenty-two months before and 27,000 nautical miles behind, just as though I had only popped into town to get some ice-cubes. It was as if no time had passed, as if no distance existed between the ice at the two poles, and Jurumirim. Yet the big coconut trees had borne new fruits and the small ones had grown up.

In the stillness of Jurumirim, listening to the distant voices from *Rapa Nui*, I stood there, waiting for them to come up so we could go to the beach. They were taking such a long time. Twenty-two months to reach the very same sand. I could have spent this time living – as I had lived before – here between the mountains of Paraty and the sea. Who knows, I could have undertaken some great exercise under the shadow of coconut trees, without having to travel 27,000 miles to feel the ice of both the South and North Poles.

But this would have served no purpose. I would have arrived nowhere. I would not have returned. And nor would I have discovered that the greatest dreams can be made of a handful of stones in a blue bag.

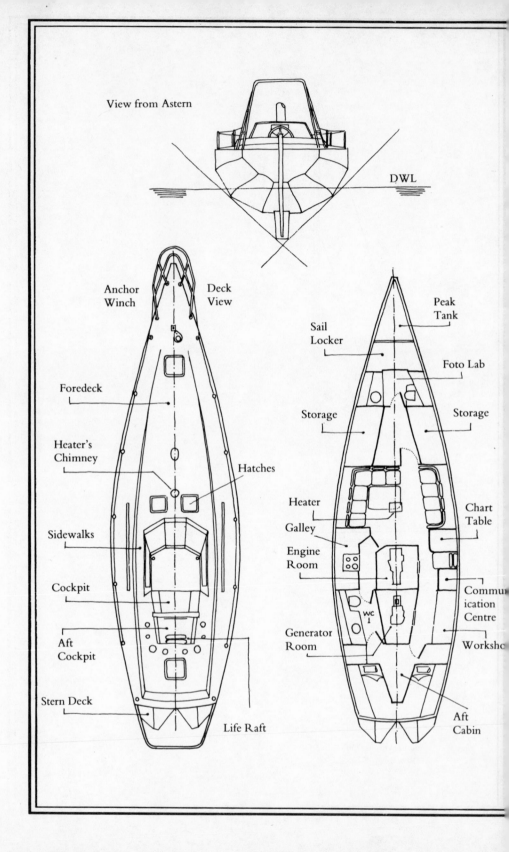

View from Astern

DWL

Anchor Winch

Deck View

Foredeck

Heater's Chimney

Hatches

Sidewalks

Cockpit

Aft Cockpit

Stern Deck

Life Raft

Sail Locker

Peak Tank

Foto Lab

Storage

Storage

Heater

Galley

Engine Room

Chart Table

Communication Centre

Generator Room

WC

Workshop

Aft Cabin

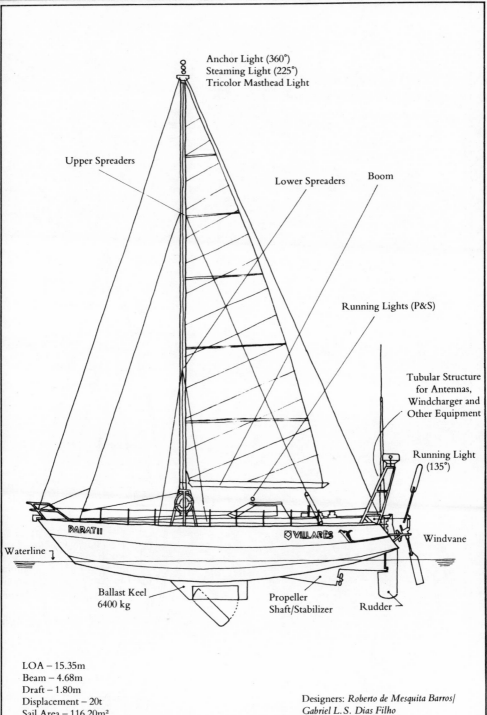

Anchor Light (360°)
Steaming Light (225°)
Tricolor Masthead Light

Upper Spreaders

Lower Spreaders

Boom

Running Lights (P&S)

Tubular Structure
for Antennas,
Windcharger and
Other Equipment

Running Light
(135°)

PARATII

VILLARES

Windvane

Waterline

Ballast Keel
6400 kg

Propeller
Shaft/Stabilizer

Rudder

LOA – 15.35m
Beam – 4.68m
Draft – 1.80m
Displacement – 20t
Sail Area – 116.20m²
Engine: Maxion Perkins – 4236M

Designers: *Roberto de Mesquita Barros/*
Gabriel L.S. Dias Filho
Assisted by: *Jean Dualibi*

ACKNOWLEDGMENTS

To everyone, companies or individuals, who sailed aboard
Paratii, and made this journey possible:

Villares Industries

Quaker Produtos Alimentícios Ltda
Nutrimental S/A Indústria e Comércio de Alimentos
Le Coq Sportif Comércio de Representação Ltda

Admiral Charles Williams, Albarus S/A Indústria e Comér-
cio, Alcan Alumínio do Brasil S/A, Alternativa Viagens e
Turismo Ltda, Álvaro Guidotti, Álvaro Ricardo de Souza,
Ana Maria Bergo Yahn, Andreas Stihl Moto Serras Ltda,
Asberit S/A, Ashraf Klink, Audichromo Editora Ltda,
Bullhoff-Dodi Sistema de Fixação e Montagem, Buniek
& Duailibi Informática Ltda, Carlos Piaggiaro, Celso
Morelli, Claudia Bertolozzi Maluf, Copagás Distribuidora
de Gás Ltda, Cordoaria São Leopoldo S/A, Décio Cezaretti,
Diretoria de Hidrografia e Navegação, Dow Química S/A,
dr Edison Mantovanni Barbosa, Edra do Brasil S/A,
Eduardo Louro de Almeida, Elebra Informática Ltda,

Empax Embalagens S/A, Fania – Fábricas de Instrumentos para Auto-Veículos Ltda, Fausto Chermont, dr Fernando Teixeira V. de Oliveira (Fêca), Flora Lys Spolidoro, Geraluz Indústria e Comércio Ltda, Giroflex S/A, Goyana S/A, Guillaumon – LGS Hidráulicos, Hanseática Estaleiros Ltda, Hélio Setti Jr, Heliodinâmica S/A, Henkel S/A Indústrias Químicas, Hering Malas S/A, Hermann Atila Hrdlicka, Hospital de Marinha do Rio de Janeiro, Indupar S/A Indústria de Paráfusos, Issao Kohara, Instituto Astronômico e Geofísico, Instituto Oceanográfico, Instituto de Pesquisas Tecnológicas – Departamento Naval da USP, Jean Duailibi, Johnson & Johnson do Brasil, José Antonio Moeller, José Carlos B. Furia, José Mário Brasiliense Carneiro, Kalil Sehbe S/A Indústria do Vestuário, Kon Tiki Museum – Thor Heyerdahl, Lauro Aidar, Levefort Indústria e Comércio Ltda, Luiz Matoso, Manuel R. Garcia, Massey Perkins S/A, Maxion S/A, Metalúrgica Detroit S/A, Metalúrgica Suprens Ltda, Mobil Oil do Brasil S/A, Nautitécnica, Nife do Brasil Sistemas Elétricos Ltda, oceanographic vessel *Barão de Teffé*, oceanographic vessel *Prof. Besnard*, Nutrimental Cozinha Experimental S/A, Nysse Arruda, Olleg Belli, Osram do Brasil S/A, dr Pirajá Guilherme Pinto, Pirelli S/A Cia Industrial Brasileira, Polar Equipamentos Ltda, René Hermann, Robert Bosch Ltda, Roberto de Mesquita Barros (Cabinho), Roberto Stickel, Prof. Rubens Junqueira Villela, Shell do Brasil S/A, Thierry Stump, Thomaz Brandolin, Thomaz Camargo Coutinho, Tintas Renner S/A, Tubos Plásticos Spiraflex Ltda, VDO Comercial Ltda, Zeca Abu-Jamra, and all the radio 'ham' community.

BIBLIOGRAPHY

AMUNDSEN, Roald, *The South Pole* (Hurst, London, 1978).

Antarctica: Great Stories from the Frozen Continent (Reader's Digest, Australia, 1985).

Arctic Pilot — Den Norske Los — Jan Mayen (Norwegian Hydrographic Service, Svalbard, 1988).

BJELKE, Rolf and SHAPIRO, Deborah, *Northern Light: Its Epic Arctic–Antarctic Sailing Voyage* (Queen Anna Press Books, Stockholm, 1986).

BOORSTIN, Daniel J., *Os descobridores* (Civilização Brasileira, Rio de Janeiro, 1989).

CHARCOT, Jean, *The Voyage of the Pourquoi Pas?* (Hurst, London, 1978).

CHOPARD, Michel, GAZANION, Daniel, MAROUX, Bruno and MONCHAUD, Claude, *Kim: Mer, Soleil, Glaces* (Éditions du Pen Duick, France, 1983).

COOK, Frederick A., *Through the First Antarctic Night 1898–1899* (Hurst, London, 1980).

FUCHS, Sir Vivian, *Of Ice and Men* (Anthony Nelson, Oswestry, 1982).

GARRARD, Apsley Cherry, *The Worst Journey in the*

World, 2 vols (Constable, London, 1922).

GERLACHE, Ct Adrien de, *Quinze mois dans l'Antarctique: Voyage de la Belgica* (Hachette, Paris, 1902).

HASSE and SCHRÖDER, Barbara M., *Iceland: More than Sagas*, (Schröders Ord & Bildbyrâ AB, Sweden, 1990).

HUNTFORD, Roland, *The Last Place on Earth*, (Atheneum, New York, 1985).

LANSING, Alfred, *A Incrível Viagem do Endurance* (José Olympio, Rio de Janeiro, 1989).

LEWIS, David and GEORGE, Mimi, *Icebound in Antarctica* (W. W. Norton, New York, 1987).

PONCET, Sally, *Le Grand Hiver* (Arthaud, Paris).

ROTH, Hal, *Two Against Cape Horn* (Penguin, Ontario, 1978).

The Antarctic Pilot (N.P.9. Hydrographer of the Navy, London, 1974).

The Vikings (National Geographic Society, Washington, D.C., 1972).

WILSON, Edward, *Diary of the Terra Nova Expedition to the Antarctic 1910/1912* (Blandford Press, London, 1972).

WORSLEY, F. A., *Shackleton's Boat Journey* (W. W. Norton, London, 1977).

A NOTE ON THE AUTHOR

Amyr Klink was born in São Paulo, Brazil in 1955
and lives in Paraty, the beautiful place between Rio
and São Paulo after which his boat is named, He has
also written *One Hundred Days Between Sea and Sky*,
an account of his Atlantic crossing in a rowing boat.

SOUTHERN ICE

SOUTH SHETLAND ISLANDS

PALMER ARCHIPELAGO

BISCOE ISLANDS

ADELAIDE ISLAND

GRAHAM LAND

ANTARCTIC PENINSULA

LARSEN ICE SHELF

Mar de Weddell
(Weddell Sea)

I. Elephant
I. Clarence
I. Gibbs
I. King George
I. Nelson
I. Roberts
I. Greenwich
I. Livingstone
I. Snow
I. Smith
I. Low
Estreito
Brandsfield
I. Bridgeman
I. D'Urville
I. Joinville
I. Decepción
I. Astrolabe
I. Trinity
I. Tower
I. Brabant
I. Hoseason
I. Danco
I. Amberes
Canal de Neumayer
Puerto
I. Lieja
I. Seymour
I. Ross
Snow Hill
I. Robertson
Canal Bismark
I. Renaud
Crüad
Sound
I. Lavoisier
I. Biscoe
R. Drygalski
B. Darbel
Gullet
R. Megunda
R. Lagunas

Pacífico Sul
(South Pacific Ocean)

CHILE

ARGENTINA

Mar de Bellingshausen
(Bellinghausen Sea)

Ushuaia
Cabo Horn
Drake Passage
Staten Island
Is. Falkland
Malvinas

BRASIL

Rio de Janeiro
Jurumirim
PARATY

Is. Orkney

Mar de Weddell
(Weddell Sea)

I. Geórgia do Sul

Is. Sandwich do Sul

Atlântico Sul
(South Atlantic Ocean)

Círculo Polar Antártico

ANTÁRTICA

+ PÓLO SUL
(SOUTH POLE)

South Africa
Cape Town

Trópico de Capricórnio
(Tropic of Capricorn)